JIM McCORMICK AND MARYANN KARINCH

Business Lessons from the

EDGE

Learn How Extreme Athletes Use Intelligent Risk-Taking to Succeed in Business

Mc
Graw
Hill

New York   Chicago   San Francisco   Lisbon   London   Madrid   Mexico City
Milan   New Delhi   San Juan   Seoul   Singapore   Sydney   Toronto

Library of Congress Cataloging-in-Publication Data

McCormick, Jim.
    Business lessons from the edge : learn how extreme athletes use intelligent risk-taking to succeed in business / by Jim McCormick and Maryann Karinch. — 1st ed.
        p.   cm.
    ISBN 978-0-07-162698-9 (alk. paper)
        1. Success in business.   2. Teams in the workplace.   I. Karinch, Maryann.   II. Title.

    HF5386.M143   2009
    658.4′09—dc22   2009002432

To each other

1 2 3 4 5 6 7 8 9 10 11 12 13 14 15 16 17 18 19 20 21   FGR/FGR   0 9

ISBN 978-0-07-162698-9
MHID   0-07-162698-0

McGraw-Hill books are available at special quantity discounts to use as premiums and sales promotions, or for use in corporate training programs. To contact a representative please e-mail us at bulksales@mcgraw-hill.com.

This book is printed on acid-free paper.

Contents

PART 2   TEAM LEADERSHIP

PART 3 TEAM EXCELLENCE

Preface

INSIDE YOUR COMFORT zone, you participate in everyday activities like walking to get coffee, driving to work, playing golf. Now open the door marked "Exit Only." Step over the threshold. The demands on your mind and body suddenly intensify. The literal version is going through the door of an airplane for a skydive: the air is colder, things happen faster, and you will experience the thrill of a lifetime. Among the benefits is emotional empowerment, cranking up that voice in your head that yells, "I did that, so I can do anything."

You have to survive the initial experience, of course, if you want to do it again or to have the benefits spill over into other areas of your life. That's where the "intelligent" part of "intelligent risk taking" comes into play.

The athlete-executives in this book do not lose sight of that all-important modifier. If all it took were guts to start a company and drive it to the top of an industry, we would see a lot of daredevils in the leagues of the billionaire business leaders.

But the people featured in this book are not daredevils. They know where the edge is because they've calculated it. They know how and when to go right up to it because they have good data sources combined with intuition that has been fine-tuned by experience and coaching.

And they have lessons that will enable you to go through the door to exit your comfort zone and do more in your life. They will tell you not only what it's like to have high ambition and fantastically active imagination but also how to put them to work through intelligent risk taking. They will show you the correlation between self-awareness and personal challenge and moving toward oneness with the financial cosmos.

With the benefit of their insights, as well as our acumen as business professionals and extreme athletes, you now have a guidebook to personal excellence, team leadership, and team excellence to help you achieve remarkable success in business.

Acknowledgments

STARTING WITH OUR inspiring editor, Ron Martirano, we thank our great team at McGraw-Hill, including Joe Berkowitz, Craig Bolt, Heather Cooper, Staci Shands, Kenya Henderson, and Seth Morris.

We appreciate the assistance of the people who helped us get connected and stay connected with the athlete-executives in this book (in alphabetical order): Meredith Ambrose, Carla Baker, Priss Benbow, Katie Bradshaw, Kary Delgado with RR Partners, David Dennis, Jamie Diaferia with Infinite Public Relations, Jane Edwards, Sarah Evans, Dena Grigas with Lages & Associates, Stacy Holand with the Women's Sports Foundation, Natalie Leung, Brie Lyall, Cassandra Marrone, Kelly McLear, Megan Murphy, Janine Nicol, Leslie Page, Kristine Peterson, Meier Raivich, Teresa Richey, Joe Sinnot, Felicia Sinusas with Jane Wesman Public Relations, Suzanne Sonnell, and Stephanie Winkles.

Our thanks to others who gave their time and insights to help the project move forward: Beth Geno, Samantha Rottenberg Karinch, Amy Love, Ross Shonhan, and Amy Vernetti. We also appreciate the help that Ellen Jacobs gave us in getting the most out of the excellent Hoover's database.

Extraordinary Is Only the Beginning

THE ATHLETE-EXECUTIVES FEATURED in this book have pushed past normal limits of human performance and, in the process, faced unpredictable circumstances. They share a unique perspective on challenge in addition to a certain kind of mental organization and physical discipline. The challenge may show up as speed, elevation, or endurance, but at its core it is simply a stimulating task, not unlike starting or taking over a company. In both the athletic and the business realms, rising to the challenge has given them opportunities to achieve something that most people find mind-boggling or impossible.

The lessons they have learned not only make an extraordinary feat a reality but also provide a blueprint for repeated success.

Like you, most of the featured executives did not have the advantage of celebrity status when they entered the world of business. While top athletes who used their fame to launch businesses often do have messages worth absorbing, the athlete-executives in this book achieved success in ways that demonstrate universally applicable lessons.

Why Do You Do This?

People commonly view going to the edge physically, mentally, or emotionally as something to avoid because they do not see themselves as capable of staying "safe enough." But that self-limiting judgment isn't something we're born with; we are socialized toward it. Fortunately, we can also be socialized out of it—we just need to expose ourselves to intelligent risk takers like the people featured in this book. They are people who see taking on extraordinary challenge as part of a set of actions leading to rewards. These actions also include effectively evaluating options, identifying opportunities, and seizing them at the right moment. This triad of success skills relates directly to the way they approach both extreme and unconventional sports and business.

In looking at why successful businesspeople pursue demanding athletic activities, we start to see how their athletic and business endeavors interrelate. These mountaineers, skydivers, race car drivers, bull riders, and other executive extreme athletes sometimes get harangued by people who can't see the point of doing what they do. Others aspire to doing those kinds of things but can't seem to get their actions to match their desires. Both types of nonparticipants ask, "Why do you do this?" but for different reasons. One group looks for a flaw in logic or emotional instability, and the other seeks the flawless logic and emotional strength that might help each of them actually take a step toward the activity.

The common answer the athlete-executives have for "why" is simple. They love what they do. That intense feeling relates to a number of interrelated, core motivations for their brand of challenge.

Self-Discovery

For some people the allure of pushing past normal limits means coming to grips with fears of the unknown and fostering the ability to handle change. A compelling reason to move out of your comfort zone on a regular basis is that you always learn more about yourself in that setting. It's a route to gaining self-insight, gauging how well you respond to adversity, and discovering ways to do it better the next time.

Good Company

Bob Gordon, the CEO of Outward Bound Professional, says he never met a climber he didn't like, and that pretty much sums up a major reason someone wouldn't just try a very demanding sport a few times and then leave it. The people who have this interest in common share mental assets and emotional drives that psychically glue them. Many of them have gone to the finest business schools in the world, founded and now shepherd successful companies, and raised families—the combination of which would fulfill most people to the extent that they didn't need to do any more. But these achievers still felt that they needed not only another dimension to their lives but also the company of others who appreciate that dimension. Regardless of their activity, they are societal explorers.

The Adrenaline Advantage

The ability to perform well under high stress provides advantages in any environment. The term *adrenaline rush*—as opposed to *adrenaline advantage*—suggests that arms and legs are moving, but not necessarily under the direction of the cognitive brain. The activities involving danger found in the challenges undertaken by people featured in this book require quick decision making in addition to moves fueled by hormones. By going to the edge again and again, they force themselves to think under stress, and that skill is quite useful when the competition has announced a revolutionary new product the same day as your meeting with potential investors.

The Competence Rush

An adrenaline rush can be a great side benefit of going to the edge, but a main motivator for many professionals is not the hormone frenzy; it's the control they maintain in intense situations. Going to the edge and succeeding because of their wits and skill thrills them to their core. The competence rush comes from the satisfaction of accomplishing something that's exceedingly difficult in both an absolute and a relative sense. As Don Bell, internationally ranked race car driver and founder and CEO of Bell Microproducts, says, "The challenge is why you do it."

Pushing Physical Limits

Many of the people featured in the pages that follow thrive on extreme physical challenges, like the recruits in boot camp who look at an obstacle course and see the finish line, not what's standing in their way. They relish chances to test their fitness and sharpen their minds in outrageous circumstances.

Don Bell,
founder, presi-
dent, CEO, and
chairman of the
board of Bell
Microproducts,
preparing for
a race

This is the mentality of a high-altitude mountaineer, barely able to push a whisper past his frozen beard at 26,000 feet, but if you could hear what he's saying, it's probably "Bring it on!"

Deidre Paknad, an avid cyclist and president and CEO of PSS Systems, interprets the challenge like this: "I ask myself, Why do I choose the harder thing? Why do I ride to be competitive with the guys with the shaved legs?" The answer: you have to climb the hills to get the stunning view from the top. And the higher the hills, the better the view. On a conscious level, she sees this as a metaphor for why she opts for the harsh demands of leading start-up companies: "I don't know how to choose the easy things. I have experience choosing the hard things—and success at it. I get nothing from choosing the simple route."

Environmental Love Affairs

These athlete-executives love the environment where they play, and the harder they play, the more they awaken to the wonders of their chosen arenas. It could be a dirt track, an air show, an unmarked slope in the backcountry, or an open ocean. These athletes not only love their playgrounds but also honor them. They consciously connect their enjoyment of risk in their surroundings with both respecting and being in touch with them. In their own way, all the people in this book have a relationship with their world that is fundamental to their athletic and business success. They don't let circumstances control them; they seek the most gratifying views.

During the course of an extreme athletic effort—whether it lasts for a few minutes or a few weeks—multiple motivators can surface, converge, and reinforce each other.

My first jump instructor, Jim Wallace, had about 8,000 skydives when I met him in 1988. His skydiving activities, as well as my seeing the U.S. Navy exhibition skydiving team jump into the Rose Bowl with the game ball and land precisely on the 50-yard line, inspired me in a specific direction in the sport: I wanted to do exhibition skydives. Jim invited me—at a jump count of 333—to join him and another colleague with thousands of skydives to be the opening entertainment for a prestigious horse show.

To say I felt significant fear is an understatement. The challenge surpassed what those Navy jumpers faced at the open arena in Pasadena because this was a standard-sized riding ring, about 100 feet by 200 feet, or roughly half the size of the landing space at the Rose Bowl. It got worse. On the left side of the ring were bleachers and an announcer's stand with wires going off to the loudspeakers. Not a good place to land. A steep slope ran along the entire right side. Not a good place to land. On another side of the ring was a white VIP party tent with caterers dashing around and linen cloths covering the many tables. Not a good place to land. On the far end were television trucks with broadcast towers sticking up. Not a good place to land. I scanned the interior of the ring, and then I really got scared. The riding jumps had already been positioned in the ring, so there wasn't an unobstructed area in sight.

At this point it became apparent to me that this would not be a normal skydive. And then Jim gave me a smoke canister mounted on a bracket. I had never seen one before and had no idea what to do with it. So in addition to the challenge of landing in this small, obstacle-filled area in front of an audience, I now had to wear a piece of hardware on my left shoe that was actually threatening. "Here's what you do if it starts to burn your foot," Jim said as part of his briefing. I had to be prepared to wear it, activate it under canopy so smoke would pay out during descent and jettison it if it malfunctioned. Oh, by the way, he mentioned (though the thought already had made it into my consciousness), don't ditch it over the crowd if there's a problem because it could seriously hurt someone.

I was emotionally overtaxed and wound tight about doing this, but I could not imagine backing out, and deep in my head I'd made a judgment that I had the skill to match my desire to succeed. That said, I think I stopped breathing and was an inch away from staying in the airplane as we approached the moment to exit.

Two minutes to the jump and we did a pass at 3,500 feet. The riding ring looked tiny at that altitude. Spectators had collected all around it. Horses were poised outside, ready to enter the ring. With each passing minute, more obstructions and obstacles came into our view. The areas where we could land safely seemed to contract as the seconds passed.

I was dry-mouthed and uncertain as we prepared to exit. Jim faced me and had his head out the door so he could spot—that is, determine—when we had reached exactly the right place to exit. He turned to me and said, "Jim, you know what?"

What else can possibly happen at this point? I thought.

"This is when I really get scared."

He may have made that comment because he knew I was on the verge of becoming nonfunctional. But for my mentor, my instructor, the guy who had brought me into the many dimensions of the sport, to acknowledge that he was frightened at this point was immensely important to me. I felt fear, but I wasn't alone in it. That gave me both a cognitive and an emotional boost. I was ready.

I had one of the best mentors in the business, and I figured I would just follow him out the door and do whatever he did. I came in over that party tent, made a left turn to avoid a riding jump, and landed successfully to the applause of the crowd.

Two days later I called Jim and asked him how we could make that happen again. We formed the Twenty-first Century Skydiving exhibition team right after that, and even though I've moved from Southern California and only occasionally join the team, the venture lives on with Jim at the helm.

Self-discovery, good company, competence rush, pushing of physical limits—they all played a role in my desire to do it the first time and do it again many, many times after that. Even the environmental love affair became part of it eventually, because I realized that few people, other than pilots and climbers, ever have a dramatic, physical sense of the three dimensions of our world. In free fall and under canopy, I have the viewpoint of an eagle.

The Passion/Life Nexus

The people who do these things are not identical personality types with analogous backgrounds, although they do have some common traits. The most pronounced of them is what I call a *passion/life nexus*. *Competence rush* or *pushing of physical limits* may describe why someone gravitates to a particular athletic effort. But the core reason for returning to the edge year after year—and why their businesses thrive with unusual energy—is this experience. If there is any aspect of their personalities and motivation that both binds them with people who are not extreme athletes and inspires anyone who comes in contact with them, it's the connection, or nexus, between their passion and how they live life. The stronger the nexus, the better the individual is at taking risks and pursuing opportunities. People on a course fueled by passion are energized.

Looking at the elements that converge to achieve that nexus tells us a lot about the people featured in this book.

The executive extreme athletes we focused on have a secure knowledge of their natural skill set in both the athletic and business arenas. That skill set comprises innate talents that they may have recognized early on or that were so obvious to the world that people around them kept saying "You're really good at that!" Having identified a natural skill set by no means suggests that a person knows exactly in which venue to apply it, however. That is where another ingredient of their success comes into play: all have searched for a sense of purpose.

People with a healthy regard for themselves and their abilities tend to think that they have a reason for being on this earth. Purpose is a heady and elusive concept, but paradoxically, it is also a grounding and simple one. The big bucket *achievement* contains myriad varieties of purpose, and a fascinating result of some of our featured executives pursuing athletic heights was that they became much clearer about their purpose in a nonsports environment.

Another unifying element relies on a combination of intelligence and open-mindedness: they found their calling. In pursuing sports and business activities that apply their natural skill set, sense of purpose, and passion, they discovered what thing, or things, they were "meant to do." They arrived at the passion/life nexus.

Another important commonality is what they are not. *Daredevil* and *extreme athlete* are not interchangeable terms. That's why the names of some high-profile businessmen do not appear in these pages. We focus on outstanding business executives skilled in intelligent risk taking—people who, for the most part, get the applause and admiration of their boards of directors rather than watching the directors cringe every time they undertake a new adventure.

We also focus on people with aspirations that positively affect people around them. That means egomaniacs and abusive control freaks—no matter how successful they are—could not sit in the company of the people we interviewed and grew to respect.

Lessons from the Edge

The lessons fall into three primary categories: personal excellence, team leadership, and team excellence. Here is a summary of how these athlete-executives did it, with the specifics coming to life in the following chapters:

Personal Excellence
Honor Your Passion
Leverage your passion to build success.
Trust that the more your work engages your passion, the
    more successful you'll be.
Give your spirit a megaphone.

Know Your Limitations
Call on others to counter your shortcomings.
Delegate with your talents and objectives in mind.
Use your self-awareness to frame your vision.

Welcome Humility
Build your personal brand.
Put ego in its place.
Don't be an end-zone dancer.
Take pride in your successes, but let other people
    celebrate you.

Exude Integrity
Be true to your moral compass.
Identify your nonnegotiables in advance.

To Be a Top Performer, Get Coached
Make up for your weak spots.
Identify role models.
Know that outside colleagues are invaluable.
Stay open to the advantages that inside colleagues can offer.
Be aware that most people are happy to share their
    insights and experiences; that's good and bad.
Look to yourself for answers.

Liberate Your Ideas
Make clarity time a habit.
Don't let your work consume you.
Give your thoughts cohesion and power.
Give life to your ideas.

Be a Stimulus for Passion
Carry and spread passion: it's a good virus.
Help people discover passion through their own ideas.
Let quality control take hold.
Live in the future.

Define Your Goals
Set goals from the inside.
Make goals real through accountability.

Be Ready to Seize Opportunity
Break the rules if you want to excel.
Know that maverick thinking does not mean wacky ideas.
Move in a timely manner; opportunities are fleeting.
Recognize the opportunity, assemble the team, and take action.

Practice Resilience
Exploit setbacks for the lessons they provide.
Analyze setbacks so you head straight to success instead of
    repeating mistakes.

Let the pain of failure help you set priorities.

Never Give Up
Live the belief that packing it in is not an option.
Know that you may need to revise your goals and methods to
    keep moving forward.
Chart your progress.
Fixate on results.

Focus Yields Efficiency
Focus at the right level.
Exercise focus to support discipline and time management.
Use your focus to help structure priorities and an action plan.
Know that focus helps you figure out what's next.
Trust that focus takes you out of panic mode.

Team Leadership

Your Team Is Critical
Never compromise on hiring decisions.
Never forget that your team is only as strong as its weakest link.
Build a Magnetic Culture™.
Give your team members permission to push back and offer their
    true opinions.
Always let your team members shine when they succeed.
Don't be afraid to hire people who are better than you.
Say "good-bye" if you must.

Abhor Mediocrity and Average Behavior
Strive to be the best—and that doesn't mean the best among
    the average.
Believe in yourself, but be reasonable; you're not a superhero.
Deliver your personal best.
Prepare for the outcome you are seeking.
Be persistent but patient.
Persevere, with a plan.
Don't kill yourself trying; make time to relax and savor.

Eliminate the Victim Mentality

Choose your associates carefully; victims are losers.

Take control of your destiny.

Know that successful professionals adapt.

Eliminate the excuses.

Grieve and then move on.

Own your mind-set.

Influence Others with Your Behaviors and Results

Lead by persuasion, not fear.

Never forget that authenticity is powerful; exhibit it by performing.

Just do it if you want others to do it too.

Create Ways for People to Achieve More as Part of the Team than by Going It Alone

Act on the truth that we all aspire to be part of something greater than ourselves.

Sell a vision.

Maintain Situational Awareness

Continually question the status quo.

Be heads-up and try to look around the corner.

Celebrate Your Victories

Make the celebrations fact based.

Match incentives to desired behavior.

Recognize successes immediately after they occur.

Reward the intelligent risk takers, even when they fail.

Give yourself a medal too.

Team Excellence

Insist on Goal Clarity

Make sure everyone is clear on the goal.

Remember that goal clarity will empower your team to make good decisions.

Establish personal goals while honoring organizational goals.

See Risk as a Tool, Not a Threat
Determine your risk quotient.
Know the difference between intelligent risks and fatal risks.
Make risk a tool to be utilized, not minimized.
Help your team discover their tolerance for risk.

Manage Risk with Contingency Thinking
Know what causes bad outcomes.
Think your way through potential disasters.

Push to the Edge
Find out what you, others, and your organization are truly capable of.
Use metrics to keep the momentum going.
Engage your imagination.

Be Fluid
Recognize that adapting is gaining strength, not compromising it.
Be sensitive to market signals.

Focus Outward
Don't try to make your life easier at the expense of your customers' and
    clients' needs, or the company will flounder.
Take a customer-centric approach to build business.
Ask yourself, "Whom are we trying to please with this change or
    initiative?"
Know that companies guided by their customers' and clients' needs
    raise the bar.

You Have to Find a Way
Make it work with what you have—resources are always limited.
Approach the challenge from a different angle.
Stay curious.

The athlete-executives you will meet in the upcoming chapters share stories that illustrate how these lessons affect business performance. Use them
and you will add to your own success stories.

PART 1

PERSONAL EXCELLENCE

CHAPTER 1

Grow Up to Be a Cowboy:

Honor Your Passion

Passion: a person's deeply held desires, concerns, and beliefs. This is not exactly the dictionary definition of the concept, but it is the one I want you to keep in mind as you read this chapter.

TY MURRAY, PRESIDENT of Professional Bull Riders, is "King of the Cowboys." He is to rodeo what Wayne Gretzky is to hockey or Michael Jordan is to basketball.

Ty was not one of those kids who wanted to be a football player one week and an astronaut the next. In a fifth-grade essay about what he wanted to do when he grew up, he wrote: "I want to beat Larry Mahan's record," referring to the six All-Around World Championships of the rodeo legend who was his hero. Ty realized that dream on December 13, 1998, when he earned a record-breaking seventh All-Around World Championship title.

The passion for rodeo pumped through his body like blood, as it did with all of the other men in his life. His father and uncle, grandpas, and great grandpas—they were all cowboys and men Ty looked up to. His grandpas put on Wild West shows in the 1920s, so they knew the entertainment value of rodeo as well. It's a realization that drove Ty to form Professional Bull Riders, an athlete-owned organization that is successfully bringing "America's original extreme sport" to homes in America and abroad through Versus (formerly Outdoor Life Network) and Telemundo.

Ty has no trouble summing up why he has honored his passion ever since he can remember: "I have loved the cowboy life—everything about it—since the day I was born. There's no other feeling on this earth like making great rides on great animals." But it's more than that. It's not just what he does but what he is: "I don't care about going down in history as a great bull rider or bronc rider. I hope people will remember me as a great cowboy."

Leverage Your Passion to Build Success

Activities we care deeply about will often correlate with things we're good at. People who can craft an occupation that leverages their passion have an enormous advantage because they are now doing something they have invested themselves in as a part of their livelihood. That's tremendously energizing.

Mark Richey is an Alpine-style climber who has done first ascents as well as climbed famous and well-established routes on mountains like Everest. *First ascent* refers to the first modern recorded climb to reach the summit of a mountain or to pioneering a particular climbing route. Climbers and mountaineers who do first ascents are true explorers; their risk factor and the level of challenge they face is much greater than for those who follow.

Mark is president of Mark Richey Woodworking, a $20 million operation, and he sees a distinct correlation between the two worlds he explores:

"In the middle of the night we were still going up, and it was calm. Not a cloud in the sky. The stars came out—there were shooting stars. It was relatively warm for 20,000 feet. Steve [Swenson] and I were climbing in the darkness with our little headlamps. There was not another human being for who-knows-how-many miles around us. It was an extraordinary place. I will never forget that.

"How does that relate to my business? From day one we focused on the highest-end work. That came from training as an architect, but also from

Kirill Tatarinov, corporate vice president of Microsoft Business Solutions, during giant slalom training at Mt. Hood, Oregon

making fine musical instruments. I was attracted to really well-made things—things that displayed the utmost tradition of pride and great craftsmanship. Just to look at things that were well made—to hold them and touch them—gave me a great sense of fulfillment to know that I could make something that someone else could enjoy and appreciate.

"So from day one we built a culture in our company of producing the highest-quality objects and interiors and staked our reputation on that. We always come back to quality as one of the hallmarks of our mission in business. I'm as passionate about woodworking and architecture as I am about climbing."

Identify the things you are passionate about and then, to whatever extent possible, incorporate them into your career. If you can't do that, then at the very least find ways to incorporate them into your life. My father has loved trains since he was a boy. His father didn't see much future in a life on the rails, though, so he encouraged my father in a different direction. After finding ways to feed his enjoyment of trains, from books to trips, my father made a bold move when he retired and invested in a private railcar. He launched a whole new career by offering "rail excursions on the Scottish Thistle," which is more than a business that reflects his passion—the car actually symbolizes his passion.

When you don't find a way to incorporate your passion into your career, you can still achieve satisfaction as long as you have focus and direction about what you are doing. I have a friend who built a financially rewarding career in real estate; it's questionable whether he's even any good at what he does, but he does make money at it. He sends his kids to private schools, takes his wife on exotic vacations, and lives in a gated community full of McMansions. And I'd have to admit that he's probably happy, even though he didn't pursue his passion of serving in the ministry—which would not have given his family the prosperity they enjoy so much. He engages his passion for religion through service to his church and the way he raises his family. Is he as happy as he could be? No. He made the choice that his wife's passion for raising a family with everything they could need or want would take precedence over his own.

If you're conscious of a choice like that, you can make it with no regrets. But don't self-sabotage by accepting that situation rather than choosing it.

People might look at my career and conclude that I have a passion for public speaking, but I don't. Speaking is a tool to express my real passion, which is helping people recognize potential in themselves that they didn't realize they had. It creates a sense of fulfillment for me. Writing this book arouses the same passion.

Maryann is writing this book too, but the process of doing it engages a passion related to mine without being precisely the same. She is thrilled with learning and subsequently imparting that knowledge to other people. She has a student/teacher relationship with the world and has structured her career such that she can maintain it and enrich it.

Trust That the More Your Work Engages Your Passion, the More Successful You'll Be

Plenty of people have thriving careers and never feel a passionate connection to their work. They are not as successful as they could be, no matter how much they earn or how much corporate power they wield.

Skier Kirill Tatarinov, corporate vice president of Microsoft Business Solutions at Microsoft Corporation, is firm about the connection between passion and success: "A person without passion cannot be successful. No matter what you do, you need to be thinking about how you can change the world, how you can touch people who come in contact with your product."

Leadership requires passion, too, he believes, because leaders have the opportunity to change the lives of people they lead. The job of a leader is to help other people grow to a better state, to give them guidance on the road toward self-actualization. "You need to be passionate about that and thoughtful about how you can help them get ahead in their personal and professional life." How you help them succeed is both an enormous privilege and a responsibility for a leader.

What if you have no passion for what you do? Kirill advises you to "do something else."

For many of us, the skill set we have naturally has nothing to do with our passion. Some of the athlete-executives casually noted that they had degrees in engineering or some area of science or humanities, but that did nothing more than serve as an entrée to finding out what they really cared about. They were good at something they had little or no interest in pursuing.

Put your skills into a matrix and rank them according to competence and fulfillment—that is, how good you are at something versus how much you enjoy it.

Think of it like this.

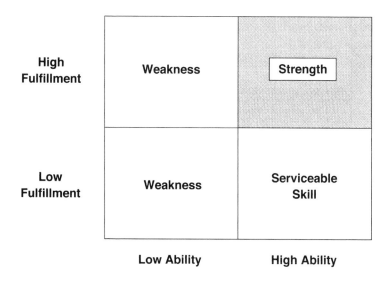

Identifying strengths as a path to engaging passions

You might find that some of the things you do best are the things that give you the least fulfillment. I hate accounting, but I aced those courses when I got my business degree. I have an undergraduate degree in civil engineering because I have an engineering brain, but I never wanted to be an engineer.

On that matrix, you know you've scored big when you see a skill show in both "high ability" and "high fulfillment."

Skills relate to your passion, therefore, but they don't define your passion.

You don't want to force yourself to try to be good at something you're not good at and, realistically speaking, will never be good at. Why frustrate yourself that way? It's one thing to know that you have a lousy golf game and may never improve much, yet go out every weekend and enjoy it, and quite another thing to drive toward being a professional golfer when you've never once made par on a hole. There are few things sadder than watching someone struggle to succeed in an area where he has no innate talent. Even if you have the best gear and the best coaches, there will always be serious limits to what you can accomplish. You might reach your peak performance; but don't quit your job and try to join the pro tour unless your best can realistically hold up against your would-be competition.

It's great to be raised with the mind-set that you can do anything you set your mind to. There comes a point, however, when you either identify your innate gifts and cultivate them to create a career aimed at self-actualization or delude yourself.

Some of the athlete-executives said that taking on extreme athletic challenges helped clarify for them what their innate talents were. The sporting challenges served as either validation of an area of competence as it related to their career or an eye-opener about their talents, depending on whether they made that discovery before or after they went into business.

Give Your Spirit a Megaphone

Troy Widgery desperately wanted to be the best, but he wasn't sure at what. He had stood on the line in midget football at age eight, pointed at the quarterback, and said: "I'd rather do that." And then he did. He had set regional track records racing his cart when he was also still in elementary school. When he connected with skydivers during his teens, though, something else happened. He liked the mental exercise, "soulfulness," and sense of independence of flying through the air. He found real passion when he connected with teammates, who actually were the best in the sport. Becoming part of a world-class team called Perris Airmoves put him at the focal point of skydiving—until the plane crash.

At 11:13 A.M. on April 22, 1992, a De Havilland Twin Otter carrying 20 skydivers and two pilots crashed seconds after takeoff. The 75-mile-an-hour nosedive into a dirt field instantly killed most of the people on board. Six jumpers—those closest to the door—survived the impact because they were hurled forward into the less fortunate people who happened to be up front. Among those surviving were three members of a nationally ranked four-way team: Dan Brodsky-Chenfeld, Tom Falzone, and Troy Widgery. Their teammate James Layne died in the crash.

Dan used to tell the team "Go slow, go slow" before exiting the plane as a way of reminding them to stay in control. It was a trigger phrase to help everyone keep body and mind at the same rate. But James would climb out of the plane and joke "Go fast."

After the crash, Troy went back to Colorado and started manufacturing the kind of helmet that could help make skydiving a bit safer. As a tribute to James, whose humor and spirit he missed, Troy told his production team to write "Go Fast" inside each helmet shell underneath the liner. That secret message helped remind them to stay focused while having fun; it became the inspiration for the Go Fast Sports product line that began with skydiving accessories and helmets and then grew to include an energy drink and energy gum.

Listen to the inner voices that shout out your passion and then respect and engage them as much as possible. And make this something you do at each stage of your career and each stage of your life.

CHAPTER 2

Flailing Means You're Not Good at It:

Know Your Limitations

KNOWING WHAT YOU do well and what you show potential to do better will get you a lot further than trying to be superior at everything you attempt. You would be better off spending that extra effort finding people whose talents complement yours and getting them in your corner.

Skydiving assaulted Diane Leopold's sense of self. At the age of 16, having worked three jobs through high school to fulfill her goal of attending college in England, Diane had built confidence that she could be good at whatever she put her mind to. This is a person who admits she "wasn't very good at math," so she earned a bachelor's degree in mechanical and electrical engineering. She still didn't quite get it, so she earned a master's degree in electrical engineering. And then an M.B.A.

It came as a surprise when she started skydiving and, for the first hundred jumps or so, was awful.

In skydiving, Diane faced something unusual—self-doubt: "I went fetal, I flailed, you name it. Being hit with the realities of not being good at something when I was a pretty confident person was a rude awakening. How could I not be OK at a sport where all you have to do is exit a plane and arch? I had to work myself through that."

Bob Travers, vice president of wealth
management for Citibank
Arden Travers

She didn't quit because she couldn't stand the idea of leaving the sport without having achieved some level of competence, but it did help stimulate thoughts about success factors that she relies on in her role as senior vice president, business development and general construction, for Dominion Resources, a $16 billion power company based in Richmond, Virginia.

"While I started out being poor at it, what ended up attracting me to it was the focus it took to do well and overcoming the mental hurdles. It was very challenging and rewarding. That's why I stuck with it. Those mental benefits certainly carried over into business.

"In business, I can't know everything. I have to surround myself with others who bring their expertise to the team. Skydiving reminded me I wasn't invincible. I wasn't going to quit until I learned how to do it, but it did provide a lesson that there are limitations to what's possible. Sometimes you have to work harder than other times."

A path to success, despite limitations, means "Get the right people involved. There are experts everywhere." And once you find them, "Promote healthy debate. Find a better way to get the job done."

Given that you will be drawing in different kinds of personalities to contribute their pieces of expertise to a plan, Diane also has guidance on how you elicit information from people who are not as confident as she is. These are the people who overestimate their limitations instead of underestimate them. For those people who fear discussion and debate, she says: "Pull them in through the discussion itself. Not by putting them on the spot, but by bringing up something that you know they have expertise in." Open the door to their information by making it clear that you not only have an interest in what they have to say, but you also need it. And then in the wrap-up on the meeting, reflect that you heard what they contributed; incorporate it into the summary. Whatever limitations you do have will be a lot less obvious when you absorb information from the experts around you.

Call on Others to Counter Your Shortcomings

Like Diane, the most successful people know what they're not good at, even though they probably hate to admit it. To the extent they find other people to contribute strengths that complement their own, they can set much loftier goals than if they went it alone.

A winning combination of talents often takes the shape of an inside person and an outside person. The inside person has the operational acumen and tactical skills. The outside one embodies the vision, develops and delivers the strategy, and serves as the public face of the company, government entity, or cause.

Richard Branson is an outside person, on the global stage building the brand of Virgin (Virgin Atlantic Airways, Virgin Records, et al.). In a March 2007 interview as part of the TED Talks with heads of state, Nobel laureates, and corporate founders in Monterey, California, he said he was dyslexic, bad at school—which he left when he was 15—and "didn't know the difference between net and gross" when he started his first few companies. With a healthy dose of humility, he gives himself some credit for success, while he gives a lot of credit to other people: "I learned early on that if you can run one company, you can really run any company. It's about finding the right people, inspiring those people, and drawing out the best in people. . . . I love to take on the status quo and turn it upside down."

Industries are not the same when Virgin enters their territory, and part of the reason is that the persona of Richard Branson comes along with the new business.

In his attempts to build and navigate a hot-air balloon capable of handling the jet stream, he ended up being pulled out of the sea by helicopters six times. "Cynics might say this is just a smart business guy executing his particular style of marketing" is the challenge he got during the TED interview. Whether or not he intended PR value in these adventures, he certainly got it. He also has done many unconventional things as the "outside man" for Virgin companies that built his personal and corporate brand.

While personality, skills, and talents all determine strengths and weaknesses, so does the situation. A good leader will not be the best leader in every environment. A great analytical mind can be unable to sort the facts under certain conditions, and that's where the inside man fits in. Stephen Murphy, an accountant who joined Virgin in 1993, has long fulfilled this role for Richard Branson at Virgin. He ascended to chief executive of Virgin Group and now heads Virgin's investment committee, roles that forced him to be a little bit more public when Virgin's big news was its move to operate like a private equity firm—a circumstance he could no doubt address more adeptly than the founder.

Many of the mountaineer-executives we interviewed subordinate their impulse to take charge whenever they are on a mountain. They hire experienced experts like Chris Warner, CEO of Earth Treks, who has summited more than 150 times on peaks above 19,000 feet, to organize and lead expeditions. They become implementers and followers on the trek with him. A veteran of Everest and one of only 305 people to summit K2 since the first ascent in 1954, Chris has a keener sense than even the most serious mountaineer-executives of managing variables like time and weather, as well as embedding a high degree of certainty related to equipment and technique. If he says, "Turn back," he means it. It doesn't matter if the guy hearing the unpleasant message is the CEO of a Fortune 1000 company; generally speaking, he will turn back if Chris says so. These mountaineer-executives have turned to Chris to make sure their alpha tendencies don't overtake the skill and judgment that is required out on a mountain. The greater an executive's self-awareness and commitment to success, the easier the transition to follower will be.

Delegate with Your Talents and Objectives in Mind

Sometimes the challenge is not finding someone who makes up for your shortcomings but rather finding someone whose talent in an area matches yours and delegating responsibility so you can make the best use of your time. Don't waste your time with something that does not engage your passion. As I said before, even though I got nothing but As in my accounting classes, I never enjoyed the subject. That's why I hire accountants.

Per Welinder displayed enormous creativity in his skateboarding, featuring a series of flat-land tricks strung together like a dance. While giving himself some credit for that ability, he feels more in tune with his "left brain" functions and makes other creative people a core part of his business team. He sees their "right brain" talents as spotlighting the path to success: "Art is very important in building brands. It brings the emotional charge to the product that gets people to see how the product is relevant to them, to say 'I want it.'"

When he first goes to the bankers or venture capitalists for backing, Per turns on the lights on both sides of his head. He knows he has to both make the financial case for a new project and stimulate an emotional buy-in with a product line while it's still in the conceptual stage. It's a great balance of science and art. But when he gets back to the office with the financing, he counts on his creative team to know how to forge an emotional connection with his customers.

Use Your Self-Awareness to Frame Your Vision

Mark Richey, the devoted Alpine-style climber and entrepreneur in architectural woodworking, says, "Rather than use equipment on the mountain to make the climb easier, [in true Alpine fashion] we try to use the skills and confidence we have to summit. But that doesn't mean you can do everything. I would not, for example, attempt K2 on a new route with a two-man team. That's unrealistic." The death-to-summit ratio on K2 is 23.8 percent for people who aren't attempting a new route, so Mark has an excellent grasp of the likely outcome.

The high-powered executives who hire Chris Warner to lead them to the top of great mountains have this self-awareness—otherwise they'd go it alone—but Chris has observed that the closer they get to the top, the more it fades.

In leading an expedition up Everest, for example, he warns the group that there may be red flags that indicate they should not proceed up the mountain. But in a private expedition, people pay a lot to be there, and they are often powerful people who are not accustomed to anyone saying "no; there's a red flag." Their default attitude is "That doesn't apply to me." They are willing to make the kind of bad decision they would never make in a business environment.

point Chris's job is to be more than a teacher; it is to be discipli-
~le reinforces the structure of the expedition in their minds, as well
as ι᷉ perception that he is the one who will make the hard decisions and
take responsibility for them: "In a perfect world, you want them to make the
same decision on their own, but as you get closer and closer to the summit,
people are willing to ignore the data because they are consumed by a desire
to get to the top. It's almost like being in an insane asylum. You have to be
the therapist—the one who makes sure they don't kill themselves." Chris
knows that if he let himself be influenced by the fact that his clients are very
powerful in other venues, he would not serve them well.

Nevertheless, some of them still want to take him on when he says "Turn
back." People do tend to thank him later, though.

An even harder call is telling a member of his team, "No, you can't go
rescue that person." It's just like when the flight attendants on a commercial
flight tell you to put the mask on yourself before you put it on a child: the
people on a mountain have to take responsibility for themselves first.

Chris tells them that part of mature self-awareness is not allowing yourself to be overcome by a heroic need. Know what you can do and stop when
you hit your limit. One of Chris's mountaineering clients is Bob Travers,
vice president of wealth management, Citi Smith Barney. Bob has observed
a striking similarity between the people on the mountain who are highly
motivated to summit—and who push each other to the summit even when
they are close to death—and people in the financial community who keep
their eyes (and their clients' eyes) on a big potential killing in the market
even when it seems to be beyond their grasp. Instead of fixating on that
prize, Bob learned to focus on the process and on risk mitigation, which is
why he abandoned the self-serving, high-risk industry standard and went
to a fee-based system of serving clients. He found everyone is more likely to
reach the summit with that approach.

Take the time to define your limitations and determine what skills and
talents people around you need to have so that your team can achieve the
goal. Letting pride push you beyond your limits is either real or virtual sui-
cide, depending on where you are at the moment.

CHAPTER 3

But Can You Backflip in the Boardroom?

Welcome Humility

THE KIND OF saintly humility some of us grew up hearing about belongs with the saints. If you build a company that provides employment, fuels the economy through services and taxes, and find time to cycle competitively and go to the park with your kids, don't say, "Oh, it's nothing." No; it's something.

The kind of humility our athlete-executives talked about gives them emotional balance and profoundly affects how other people see them. Some top executives obviously don't care what others think of them; they exhibit a lack of empathy and need for human connection that might lead some people to consider them psychopaths. Others lacking a centering type of humility are simply boisterous, self-congratulatory, tireless self-promoters. Either way, not good company.

Humility is actually a very powerful tool for people who aggressively seek success: when you allow your accomplishments to speak for themselves, you are likely to try to accomplish greater and greater things so they have a bigger and bigger voice.

Carey Hart is a superstar of freestyle motocross. His father bought him his first motocross bike when he was four with the hope of spending quality time with him, but Carey got hooked, and the father-son pastime turned into his passion. In 1998 Carey led the way in making freestyle motocross a sport worth watching and worth money to the people who participated and the companies that sponsored it. He has invented the most extraordinary moves the sport has ever seen, even becoming a featured part of "Ripley's Believe It or Not!"

Carey's head didn't swell even as his collection of medals and firsts grew through the years. Despite the feats that distinguished him forever from every other person in his sport, he knew that a backflip on a 250 cc bike meant zero in a business environment. As a business owner, he knew he had to stay true to his focus and direction, and fortunately, he had the good sense and humility to realize that he could do that only with the help of people who could do the equivalent of that backflip in the boardroom.

Carey credits his dad with teaching him how to go about pursuing success in every venue: "I get my work ethic from my dad. He's always kept me very humble and grounded. I grew up a construction worker's kid, and I still am. I'm not going to get all wrapped up in a bunch of crap about 15 minutes of fame."

Build Your Personal Brand

When you are sitting in a room with 20 people, personal brand is how the other 19 see you. Your personal brand is what you're known for, both inside and outside your company.

In a business setting, it's the job of the public relations person to build the executive's brand externally, to shape outgoing information in such a way that the public associates a certain personality, skill set, and accomplishments with that individual. It's not an easy job, but it is easier when the spin is going in the same direction as the person being spun. It's a horrible job when that is not the case, but it can still be done effectively by placing articles highlighting accomplishments and acts of goodwill, as well as sharing charming anecdotes, massaging quotes, and making the best of photo opportunities consistent with the overall message.

We made a conscious decision in this book to interview all of the people who are featured, including most of the people whose contributions take up just a line or two. That's because we didn't want spin that did not match the person's authentic personal brand. In working with a lot of PR professionals on staff at companies as well as at PR firms serving the athlete-executives who made it into the book, we found no mismatches between the people we interviewed and the way that the PR person projected their brand through initial briefings.

Your personal brand goes well beyond how the public or anyone external to the company perceives you. It is internal—how your colleagues see you, everything that you are known for on a day-to-day basis.

Freestyle motocross star Carey Hart

I recently spoke to a chief executive who had a unique problem related to this. He described the company as having an ethos of operational excellence, which made it hard to do something less than perfectly. That corporate culture makes it tough for an individual to innovate because innovation brings occasional mistakes. He admitted that he has tons of ideas for improving the company, but with the organizational drive toward flawless performance so consistent, he asked, "What should I do? Not care about the expectations?"

I said no. He and his colleagues had a lot of shared emotional investment in that corporate culture, so it would not serve him to dismiss it. I suggested that he incorporate "innovator" into his personal brand, that he become the person that everyone knows as the one plugged into the balance between operational excellence and innovation.

Put Ego in Its Place

For a long time ego held Sophia Le back from accomplishing all she was capable of. Refusing to go to clinics for soccer meant that her soccer skills hit a plateau. The attitude carried over into other sports and even into the early days of her marketing communications career. And then Sophia, the marketing communications manager for Kovarus, made a breakthrough with skateboarding.

When she started skateboarding, she was too scared and too embarrassed to try anything. She didn't want anyone to see her fall. Then at one point she just realized "they fall too." To keep progressing, you have to fall. It's all part of learning that trick so you can feel accomplished. In realizing that "they fall too," Sophia also realized that "they" could not only teach her how to fall better but also how to do the tricks better. Waking up to that possibility helped her seek advice. Ironically, she started to see more of what she was capable of by admitting that she knew less: "I realized how much help from others can accelerate your learning and growth. When you don't know something, you have to ask."

If she doesn't know how to do something at work, and can't teach herself how to do it, she follows a process: (a) asking her peers, (b) getting insights from her leaders at the company, and (c) going outside the company to someone who has the experience and track record that is relevant.

Don't Be an End-Zone Dancer

"When you see teams that are really good turn into a bunch of end-zone dancing egotists, that's a waste of talent. I admire the player who, instead of dumping his helmet on the ground and jumping up and down with a look-at-me attitude, goes back to the huddle to figure out how to make another first down."

That's how Ty Murray, the most accomplished rodeo athlete in the century-long history of the sport, keeps it real. His football reference captures an image that most American sports fans have seen on a regular basis: the guy who acts like doing his job rates a fireworks display.

When people don't appreciate what you've done or think it is significant, anything short of tying them to a chair and forcing them to listen to a list of reasons why your accomplishments are a big deal will most often pr futile in changing their mind. You can subtly allude to the positive impact of your actions, but if you go beyond that you just slip into a sales role. To the extent that you simply reference past successes without fanfare, allowing those who find them interesting the opportunity to probe more deeply, you will successfully draw people into knowledge of your accomplishments without ever making an effort to spotlight them. They come more than halfway into your territory, showing more outward enthusiasm for your success than you ever have in the conversation.

Take Pride in Your Successes, but Let Other People Celebrate You

People tend to undervalue the things that come readily to them. Other people make a fuss that seems, in the mind of the achiever, disproportionate to the accomplishment. It's easy to value things that come easily a lot less than the abilities you have to work hard to acquire. Watch for this: if a strength comes to mind and your immediate thought is "Oh, that's no big deal," you've found an ability you undervalue.

Modesty is not necessarily desirable, but gratitude and humility are.

"There are ways to teach and lead without being obvious," says Sharon Kovar, a world-class extreme runner who is former manager of succession planning and development at the $225 billion Chevron Corporation. Before going to Chevron, Sharon created the training network at the Gap for both product and sales, starting out as one person with a staff of three and leaving with a staff of 30 after three years. She worked with Ken Blanchard to customize his situational leadership model to the Gap and retrained everyone from executives to store managers in the resulting principles—a unique program for the retailer during a period of transition in which brand consolidation was a dominant concern. It addressed features and benefits of a product, how you sell it, what goes in the product books, what a person does on the floor to sell to a customer—everything was done through her department. In short, Sharon streaked up the corporate ladder, partly because she is compelled by the philosophy "You have to have a healthy discontent for the way things are." Compound that with her innate ability to teach and lead and you have a success formula. But this ability to question the status quo while engaging people in the process of improving circumstances is a strength she sometimes took for granted because so much of it came naturally to her.

At 45, Sharon's victories in extreme running have served as a healthy reminder that she has the right to take pride in her business success as well and that there are good reasons why colleagues want to celebrate her success. In 2007 alone, she ran 11 races, 3 of which were ultramarathons. Among other things, she placed first for women in a 100K desert race in Tunisia and second in a 100-mile race in Namibia.

The Merriam-Webster online dictionary defines *humble* in terms of what it is not: "not proud or haughty: not arrogant or assertive." But think of humble for what it is: for an accomplished individual, it is a state of emotional balance that enables other people to appreciate you because you deserve it and work with you because they want to.

CHAPTER 4

Don't Bail Your Board:

Exude Integrity

TWIN SISTERS IZZY and Coco Tihanyi have surfed since childhood, going back before it was cool for girls to ride the waves. When Izzy grew up, she developed a method for teaching her fellow students at University of California at San Diego to surf. Her enormous success led the sisters to launch Surf Diva in 1996, a school that has grown steadily since and now includes classes in Costa Rica.

The method they built their business on begins with surf etiquette.

If a big wave is coming toward you, you might think to bail your board— meaning you jump off it and let it fly. Wrong. You want to protect yourself at all times, and if you let your board go, you jeopardize yourself, but you could also hit somebody else. An 8-foot board with an 8-foot leash puts anyone within 16 feet in danger. In fact, when in doubt about what to do, respect the ocean's unpredictable and unforgiving nature and don't add to the challenge by doing something that could drown other people. Hold on to your board and take the hit from the wave—and it will take every bit of strength you have to hold on—or that board could hit someone in the face.

The lesson from Izzy and Coco: unethical or discourteous behavior in business will give you the same outcome. People won't forget that. They don't like being hit in the face with an 8-foot board, and neither will you if you're the one it comes back to.

There are three main reasons for living with integrity. One has a touch of idealism associated with it, but two are blatantly practical in terms of your business and reinforce the message "don't bail your board."

Be True to Your Moral Compass

Since 1987, Chris Warner has led expeditions in the Alps, Africa, the Andes, the Himalayas, North America—he's been on top of nearly every high point around the world. In all of those adventures, he has never lost a single climbing partner or client. That's thousands of people. At the beginning of a private expedition he will tell his clients, "I don't work for you; I work for your mother. If I have to turn you back on the way to the summit, you will hate me, but your mother will love me. If something goes wrong and you're injured or die, your mother will never forgive me. She will make my life worse than you ever could."

Chris has also created a successful business rooted in his skills and passion and built on "principles of my mountaineering life that I bring into my business life." He founded Earth Treks, offering climbing gyms and instruc-

Mark Richey's photo of the second bivouac on the north ridge of Latok I in Pakistan, which remains one of the great unclimbed challenges in the Karakorum
Mark Richey, 2007

tion in multiple locations, as well as the private expeditions to the world's highest peaks. His business decisions related to growth opportunities reflect his long-term view of things—that is, getting there is not the point; it is how you get there. It's a case of balancing hard work with the right amount of investment and having a plan to get to the top without anyone "dying" of either exhaustion or financial blood loss. There is a huge opportunity right now in the indoor climbing industry to become the first national chain. Chris constantly hears unsolicited advice about partnering with this guy or that chain or just following the plan of so many health clubs: build up a lot of membership revenue to establish a positive cash flow and then sell to a private equity firm. Chris tells his team: "If we do this, we satisfy one part of our personality, which is the hyperambitious self. But does it create a sense of imbalance that violates who we are and what we want to experience with our families?"

Through his skill and wits, Chris has lived and led others to safety when others have perished on the same day on the same mountain. Some of those people on neighboring expeditions died because their "teammates" stepped right past their failing bodies. Chris is more than a little disgusted when he says, "Some people are so desperate to get to the summit that they make the attempt with a loose federation of partners who are not there for them in their time of need. These people adopt an every-man-for-himself attitude at a certain elevation, which is a complete violation of the spirit of mountaineering."

Chris would like to see them replace their pocket compasses with a moral one: "It's not about collecting peaks over 19,000 feet or the seven summits—whatever yardstick you want to use. Why—how—could someone choose to leave his partner in an obvious moment of need? You can get over the disappointment of not summiting, but can you ever get over the disappointment of having caused the loss of life?" (The seven summits are the highest mountains on the seven continents, generally designated as Kilimanjaro, Denali, Elbrus, Aconcagua, Carstensz Pyramid, Vinson, and Everest. They are not the hardest mountains to climb in the world; they are simply the highest in those different geographic locations.)

In interview after interview, very wealthy and ambitious people talked about the absolute necessity of behaving with integrity. One aspect of their message is that, if you compromise your reputation, you die "bankrupt." Revisit the discussion of personal brand in Chapter 3. Low integrity as part your personal brand undermines everything else you stand for. Right now, think of the celebrities in business, entertainment, sports, or politics who have reinforced very negative images over the years. They may be brilliant and capable people, and therefore continue to reap financial rewards, but they are the people that others love to hate. As a society we generally don't mind enjoying whatever they have to offer, whether it's a product or a great movie, but we sure would not want to have them around a lot. One wonders, Who does? Business, entertainment, sports, and politics are all human systems, so the humans in them who are "different"—in this case, either mindlessly or consciously ignoring their moral compass—stick out like dead trees in a healthy forest.

Without integrity, your ability to function in business can be impaired too. People are naturally reluctant to do business with someone whose commitments are questionable. The person without integrity becomes far less effective in many business settings than he or she could be.

The third reason is the most practical of all. If you operate with less than full integrity, sooner or later it will catch up with you. I have met many people in business that I felt struggled with doing things on the up-and-up, but they did because they were smart enough to realize that cutting ethical corners would put them in a bear trap later.

The mortgage mess of 2008 showed that plenty of people were willing to compromise their ethics for greed. You even heard some of them use some version of "Everybody's doing it"—a phrase that justifies nothing. They focused squarely on not missing opportunities to profit and felt they would look foolish unless they did what everyone else was doing.

To the extent that you can think through what is and is not acceptable when you're not under pressure, you should have a clear course of action once you are confronted with a morally complex situation.

One of the most formative experiences first-ascent mountaineer and company founder Mark Richey had early in his career was while he was working for William Dowd Harpsichord. He was at it late in the day, painting a harpsichord. Everyone else had already gone home. To save a little time in cleaning the paintbrushes, he flipped some of the excess paint on the brushes out the window. The next morning a neighboring businessman came in and complained to the foreman. One of the employees' cars had been under that window, and it was spattered with paint. The foreman said, "Couldn't have been one of us." Mark realized it had to have been his fault, so he admitted that he had caused it, knowing that doing so could cost him his job. He was earning minimum wage at the time, so they went easy on him and let him spend the rest of the day cleaning the car. In his head, the only voice he'd heard was the one that insisted, "Must tell the truth. Must take responsibility."

That foreman was later in a position to help Mark when he was starting his business. He gladly gave references and let him use equipment he needed. Mark's lessons out of this: Be honest. Show integrity. There is real benefit to that behavior, and you will find it.

Bill Baker, president emeritus of the most watched public television station in the country, Educational Broadcasting Corporation in New York, had to make delivering unpleasant truth a daily practice, both in the office and on the air. He says that one of the greatest challenges of media professionals is "telling people what they don't want to hear." Part of why he was personally successful, and why his station gained distinction and respect, is that he did exactly that: he told people what they didn't want to hear. Integrity was integral to his accomplishments.

Rules Versus Integrity

There can be a difference between following the rules and showing integrity; it depends on the source of the rules. You have a requirement to follow government laws and regulations. Not doing so shows a lot more than zero integrity, and there are plenty of judges who would be happy to remind you of that. There are lots of other rules, however, that seem made to be broken. Following them mindlessly will dry up the innovation inside you. One example is the demand to produce call reports to meet an arbitrary deadline set by your sales manager when you need to be out making sales. At some point the call report must be generated, but when an administrative regulation like that conflicts with productivity, it's a rule that can be broken.

A great example of "Integrity is what you do when nobody's watching" came through in my conversation with climber Mark Richey. Alpine-style climbing does not rely on fixed ropes, among other things. It is a purer style of climbing that minimizes the use of equipment. I asked Mark, if he were climbing alone and hit an impassable stretch on the pitch, would he turn back and try another pitch or go against the Alpine ethos and use aids to continue upward? Regarding the use of aids, he said, "If I did it, it would undermine my whole purpose for being there. All I had worked toward for years. I'd have to go home knowing I didn't abide by my own standards."

Deidre Paknad puts that sentiment into a business context: "Ethical compromises are just plain cheating. I want to win fair and square." It's the mantra of a classy, world-class competitor in any venue. A loss in reputation due to ethical compromises can jeopardize your ability to do business, just as doing steroids can jeopardize your ability to compete in an Olympic event. Also, the long-term cost of cutting corners in ethics is that customers will catch on and seek out someone else to deal with.

Identify Your Nonnegotiables in Advance

To summarize the three reasons to conduct yourself with integrity, you do it to:

- ◆ Stay true to your moral compass
- ◆ Establish that you can be trusted in a business deal
- ◆ Protect your reputation

If you accept those reasons, what nonnegotiables do you need to establish to achieve those objectives? That is, how do you define your own integrity? General examples of nonnegotiables would include the kinds of business dealings you would hate to encounter in others: willfully misrepresenting facts, capabilities, and statements and overpromising while underdelivering.

Very simply, stay true to what you know to be right and get that clear in your head with as much specificity as you require to adhere to a strategy of integrity. If you don't know what's right, you have bigger problems than we can address in this book.

You do yourself a favor by identifying the things on which you will not compromise. That way the decision is easy when you are confronted with an ethical conundrum. You have already established your own personal code of ethics before the temptation to compromise presents itself, and that makes it easier to make the right decision in the heat of the moment.

CHAPTER 5

Crash Alone or Win with a Voice in Your Head:

To Be a Top Performer, Get Coached

HOW DO YOU make sure you don't fall into the abyss? If you have a strong drive to succeed, you may need help calibrating your assertiveness. An unwavering focus on a goal can cause you to miss subtle signals that you're veering off course. There are countless other ways you might head toward catastrophe, and the whole time you think you're bound for the medal stand. You have three sources of excellent coaching available to you:

- Professional coaching
- Coaching from colleagues
- Self-coaching

Guidance from professionals and senior people who have experience and accomplishments to share can accelerate your development, but so can advice and insights from trustworthy peers. Because I serve as a coach to senior executives, I can share some steps in the process that will support you

ng if you would like to start there. You will get better at it with
∴, as a lot of the athlete-executives in this book have learned, their
spu.   e as excellent routes to learning key life and business lessons.

Having really good coaching is the best protection against crashing and burning. Mike Angiulo is an aerobatic pilot and paraglider, as well as the general manager of the Microsoft Office Project Business Unit. He relies on all three sources, depending on his needs at the moment. As Mike points out, aerobatics coaches don't typically say, "Good job." They say, "You were one degree off," or offer you a sense of improvement afterward by simply saying, "You were half a degree off." After winning the Northwest Regional Champion award for aerobatic flying in 2003, Mike went to Pylon Racing School at the Reno Air Races, where he participated in the pilot qualification school. It involved close quarters aerobatics, flying below 100 feet, and a whole series of other maneuvers to qualify him for wingtip-to-wingtip racing. It gave him plenty of opportunities to be half a degree off.

Part of the Reno Air Races ritual is that participants go into a room called the Room of Hard Benches. Keep in mind that people do die in air races, and it isn't just occasionally. In this room everyone politely but directly comments on everything observed, even if this means having to be critical of fellow pilots. Everyone knows that every person out there is at risk and that offering input that helps someone correct the tiniest error could save lives later.

You need that kind of forum and that kind of objective measure, whether it's created by one person or multiple people. And it may be different people and different numbers of people depending on the occasion.

Mike found it much harder to accept coaching in business than he did in the obvious life-and-death adventure of aerobatics: "I didn't want to talk to someone I saw as a glorified counselor telling me about leadership when I am the one leading a billion-dollar business and they're giving seminars. And then I realized that Tiger Woods has a coach. Tiger Woods's coach can't golf as well as Tiger. That's not his job. So in business, you form key relationships with people who are peers and mentors, but I also have a dedicated coach, who will objectively help me review priorities and review the logs in my Outlook calendar. He'll remind me of where I've spent my time in relation to what I established as my priorities and give me insights I can use. He will call me on it: 'You said recruiting top talent is your main priority, but you spent only 2 percent of your time on it.' 'You said managing poor performers is a lower priority and you spent 20 percent of your time on it.'

"He'll say, 'Mike, you're half a degree off'—and I get it. If you don't have somebody doing that work for you, you're missing something."

Mike's administrative assistant helps with the time-management portion of the process, and this is where self-coaching picks up. Her reports on how he has allocated time for in-person and phone meetings provide important performance data.

Stacie Blair, CEO of the Pacific Group, climbing at the Pinnacles in California

Make Up for Your Weak Spots

Unlike other athlete-executives we talked with, motocross innovator and champion Carey Hart did not have a coach during his years on the professional circuit. Who was better than he in execution? No one. Who had a better sense of potential tricks? No one. There was no precedent in his life or his sport for establishing a coaching relationship, but when he left the arena he was smart enough to know what he didn't know. While he could get on a bike and invent a sport, and then reinvent it every time he competed, he knew that mentality probably wouldn't guide a prudent investment strategy. He credits his business success completely with surrounding himself with competent professionals: "I have a good foundation of people around me." They serve as partners, coaches, and mentors in an environment where many of his innate talents are not applicable.

Marathoner Dennis Sponer is a lawyer by training, so in founding Scrip-Net he was like Carey—looking around for the talent that could complement his natural orientation and supplement his skills. Primarily he looks to his wife, who holds an M.B.A. and "pulls me back from the craziness in business that might cause setbacks." They started the business together; their offices are side by side. She runs the operations; he's out with the customers working on sales and customer retention.

The value of a coach is not only the knowledge the person brings to the situation but also the objectivity about both the situation and the individual being coached. You can also get coached by listening to others, watching them, and realizing what not to do. As Versus TV head Gavin Harvey says, "I have learned from the best and the worst. Everyone is a potential source of insight."

When climbers like Mark Richey attempt first ascents, the role of the coach may be simply to serve as another set of trusted eyes looking at a virgin rock face and offering intelligent observations about what the climbers might encounter. The advice cannot be specific because no one has attempted the climb before, but it can enhance the climber's contingency thinking and other elements of preparation.

In the world-record environment for skydiving, it is very common to ask others on the record attempt for advice on exiting an aircraft that is new to you, for example. When I went to Thailand in 2006 for the record attempts involving 400 skydivers, I was in the minority in terms of skydivers on the team who had never exited a Hercules C130. This four-engine military transport plane generally carries trucks and supplies around the world rather than skydivers. European military are more inclined than American military to let civilian jumpers use C130s, which is why some of us from the United States had a little disadvantage in this area. With the plane flying at 200 miles an hour, and 80 jumpers diving from the aircraft in close proximity to one another and to the propeller wash, you can get seriously hurt exiting that kind of aircraft if you don't know how to do it correctly. To give you a sense of perspective, I'm used to exiting an aircraft that can slow down to about 85 miles an hour before we leave.

So after 2,400 jumps, I had to go to people around me and admit that I was a beginner in terms of the Hercules exit. And it's a good thing I sought help, because their instruction countered everything I knew about how to exit a tailgate aircraft. If I'd just done what I thought was right, I would likely have dislocated my shoulder and been tossed around in the propeller blast like a feather in high winds. This happened to some others on the team.

In my business, too, I've had to come to grips with my limitations many times and find out quickly who among my mentors had the answer to a pressing question. The first time I did a presentation involving image magnification, so that live video of me was being projected onto huge screens, I asked a speaking coach if I had to do anything differently. Be more contained in your gestures, she said, because you will be seen by those 700 people in a larger-than-life scale, and moving your arms too much will look like flailing. They will be able to see your face for a change, though, so use it. In contrast to that, without the magnification in an audience of 700, you want to be expansive with your gestures so that the folks in the back feel as though they are part of the action.

Coaches often have a proactive role, too, in that they don't just wait for you to ask a question; they tell you what question you should be asking. They can provide astute observations to alert you about what you don't know. This is also the main reason organizations hire business consultants.

Identify Role Models

Sometimes role models rise up like saints and inspire you from the moment you meet them. This was a bit like Kirby Best's experience with one of his fake "uncles," the amazing John "Scruffy" Weir, who was one of the four Canadian pilots who spent years digging tunnels so he and his fellow POWs could escape a prison camp in World War II. His is the story of *The Great Escape*. When Kirby was very young, Uncle Scruffy taught him "Never have a regret in life. You never want to be at a place in life where you say, 'Gee, I wish I'd done that.'" Kirby, who has competed in eight different sports internationally and was on the Canadian ski and bobsled teams, says he's lived by that in sport and business. Kirby is the former CEO of Ingram Lightning Source, the subsidiary of Ingram Industries Inc. that provides print-on-demand services and currently heads up the company he founded called Performance Sleepwear.

And then there are the role models who are not so welcome at first, whose example and dominant spirit affect much of your success for years and years. Like the father of world-class water-skier and New York real estate executive Camille Duvall-Hero. Camille's parents both had a strong connection to waterskiing; in fact, they met on a waterskiing date. But Camille did not become one of *Sports Illustrated*'s "100 Greatest Female Athletes of the Century" and winner of 15 U.S. waterskiing national titles by allowing her genes to take hold. She did not passionately pursue speed on the water early on either. As far as she was concerned, waterskiing was a frightening sport, and she wanted to say "No, thanks."

"I hated waterskiing as a kid. I would ski 15 feet and then drop the rope. My dad said, 'You have to hang on to the rope.' I said, 'No,' because it scared me." Dad gave her an ultimatum: ski or I'll leave you here in the middle of the lake. She dropped the rope again, and her dad said, "See ya!" and took the boat back to the shore. There she was, in the middle of a South Carolina lake, glad to take the rope and ski back toward shore when her dad returned with the boat. She never let go again. She grew to love the sport and to appreciate her dad as a role model in skiing and as a trainer and mentor. "Dad was an engineer, and his style of training is probably why my brother and I dominated the sport from the moment we hit the competitive circuit."

Camille says her business mentor, Warburg Realty Partnership president Frederick Peters, "throws her a rope" all the time by giving her specific insights into tough deals. For example, in the high-end real estate market in New York brokers commonly have the challenge of matching clients to building "character." Existing shared owners of the building may decide they want tenants of only a certain social status, financial stature, or club membership—but that's an unwritten criterion. Knowing that before you try to shoehorn someone into a building makes the process much smoother.

Know That Outside Colleagues Are Invaluable

Shellye Archambeau, CEO of MetricStream, strongly agrees on the principle of relying on peer advice from outside her industry. Shellye leads a group called CEO Forum, for female CEOs in Silicon Valley. This networking organization for women building and leading high-growth companies gets together once a quarter with an experienced CEO to talk about operational issues, but it also has an ad hoc, informational component that is ongoing. The 14 women who belong to the forum exchange e-mails and calls regularly.

Shellye has built her company into a market leader in enterprise-wide quality and compliance management for global corporations and does not hesitate to evangelize about the practical value of coaching for mature professionals: "I encourage people to get mentors on two fronts. People commonly offer the advice that seeking mentors early in your career helps you jump-start it. I've found that involving mentors after your career has progressed might have even more value. Your questions have specificity and direction."

Marathoner and climber Dennis Sponer, founder and president/CEO of ScripNet, belongs to a forum of entrepreneurs that meets once a month. In his case, just as in Shellye's, even when the peers come from dissimilar industries there is a lot to learn and share because of the commonality of personnel and other fundamental business issues running across industries.

Mountaineer and investment banker Guy Downing sometimes finds his peers in less conventional places: "The sport attracts many highly motivated, entrepreneurial individuals, and I have established many personal relationships high on the side of some mountain on the other side of the world that have translated into successful business relationships." He draws an analogy between the types of high performers he met earning his M.B.A. at Stanford and the kind of people who aim to summit the world's highest mountains. "These are people with a primary other career, like me, who have the audacity to look at a mountain like Aconcagua and say, 'I'm going to get to the top of that.'" You surround yourself with people like that and you're bound to rise to the challenge.

Stay Open to the Advantages That Inside Colleagues Can Offer

Dennis Sponer says he has also "gotten good at hiring seasoned, experienced executives. I used to hire young, energetic people," but now he has seen the people who have experience that he doesn't and learning rewards to the company have been consistent: ScripNet was ıc. 500 three years in a row, the *Inc.* magazine ranking based on percentage growth in company net sales over a five-year period.

Dennis notes that one of the other things about hiring that mountain climbing has instilled in him is the need to take decisive action. "When you're on a mountain and the weather changes, you need to be able to assess the situation quickly—and turn back if necessary. One always wants to get to the summit, but you can't let that drive you when it's simply a bad decision to keep going. It's the same with employees. I always want to try to salvage the employee. I make excuses for bad employees. But in the end I've found that it's always better to let them go quickly."

A key point is that you can't learn anything good from a bad employee, and sometimes that person's behavior has the potential to "coach" colleagues toward her own negative conduct.

"One year ago, one of my top managers let me down in a big way. We're big on honesty at ScripNet, and I found that she had been dishonest with me. I made the typical excuses about how good she was in other ways and about how difficult it would be for the company to let her go moving forward. This was on a Friday. But then on Sunday I went for my long run, and with that came clarity. By the end of the run, I came to the only logical conclusion: she had to go. This is a living example of my favorite Wallace Stevens quote: 'Perhaps the truth depends upon a walk around the lake.'" Everyone on staff deserved better than a colleague who demonstrated how to succeed through dishonest actions.

Some companies have an even more formalized way than ScripNet's of providing in-house peer-to-peer coaching.

Waterskiing champion Camille Duvall-Hero is a managing director with Warburg Realty Partnership, the oldest real estate firm in New York. It's been around since 1896. The focus of this boutique-sized, 160-broker firm is high-end residential real estate, with average transactions running from $6 million to $8 million; it holds its own in a market where the main competitors have hundreds and in some cases thousands of brokers. Along with the purview of a firm like Warburg go interactions that are often quite political in nature, such as dealings with the boards of cooperatives, or co-ops, in which each tenant is a shareholder in a corporation that owns the building. There are also lots of quasi-social arrangements affecting high-end residential real estate transactions—as alluded to earlier in the chapter—so the intricacies of networks and relationships are as fundamental to deal making as having a keen sense of market conditions.

At the invitation of the company president and mentor, Frederick Peters, Camille participates in 90-minute meetings of the fifteen top brokers once a week. The president lobs questions at them, and everyone listens to one another's take on the question. At the end of the meeting Peters summarizes the vital bits of information related to "finger on the market, know what's happening, know what brokers are thinking, know what buyers and sellers are thinking, and listen to the marketplace." He distills all the information and disseminates it to the rest of the company. In other words, those 15 top performers are his market intelligence.

The relationships that those 15 people have constitute peer coaching in a traditional sense, according to Camille: "If you have a problem, then six people in the room will come up with a solution for you." The coaching of people in the rest of the company, however, does not fit the traditional model. True, their information does help the rest of the brokers gain advantages in the marketplace. The wrinkle is that those 15 people compete for deals against not only brokers in other companies but also people in their own company, whom they are, in effect, coaching. This is familiar coaching territory for Camille, who spent much of her waterskiing career training with primary competitors, specifically Australians Bruce and Toni Neville and the great Swiss water-skier Marco Bettosini—not to mention her own brother. Without reservation, they all helped each other through constructive criticism, even though they knew that doling out advice could result in the other person's gaining the edge in competition or setting a world record. Camille says their "tournaments during training were more intense than actual competition." They even made a game out it: the weekly loser would have to fuel the boat or make dinner all week.

The results of unbridled collegial coaching have proven phenomenal for Warburg in general and for Camille specifically, who has earned the Real Estate Board of New York's "Deal of the Year" award among other distinctions.

Be Aware That Most People Are Happy to Share Their Insights and Experiences; That's Good and Bad

If you take everyone's criticism, you will always be second-guessing yourself. And if nobody criticizes you—if the only people you let near you are the ones who are telling you positive things—then you're just blindly moving forward at risk.

Never hesitate to ask for advice, but vet your source before you ask. Early in my speaking career other speakers and some audience members would say, "Can I offer you some advice?" I used to say yes, but then I quickly learned to say, "No. I have people in my career who coach and advise me, and I'm going to leave it to them to assist me."

Multiple unvetted sources result in conflicting advice and confusion; plus they may project their goals and values onto you. You don't always want to ask your big brother and sister whether or not you should date a particular person.

The credentials of the person wanting to offer advice may impress you and everyone around you, but that person still may be a mismatch for you and your needs. In her literary agency, Maryann often has first-time authors proudly submit manuscripts that have been edited by college professors. On paper, they appear to be good choices because they hold credentials in literature. In reality, they may not know how to shape their grammatically correct sentences into a commercially viable project.

Who is well positioned to give you the best advice? Someone who has been there before. Someone whose advice has helped someone else achieve success in your area. Someone who does as much listening as talking to find out what your primary needs and concerns are, as well as what it is you already know. Someone who is a genuine supporter and wants to see you succeed or may even benefit from your success. Someone worth trusting who has earned your respect.

Mountaineer Chris Warner, CEO of Earth Treks, thinks you might also be well advised to look beyond yourself in a greater sense: "Look outside yourself for the wisdom. Realize there is a higher authority. If you don't, in a moment of weakness you might summit instead of going back to Camp 4, and you might never come back." Chris's friend and client Bob Travers was on a Kilimanjaro climb—definitely not one of Chris's—and experienced this: "I saw guides *pushing* clients onward. These clients were extremely sick, throwing up continually, weaving around, disoriented, and looked like death. Their emotions were so strong that it clouded their judgment as they told the guides to keep pushing them onward. I told one of those individuals to turn back, but they kept going. That night one of these people died."

Be careful whom you listen to.

Look to Yourself for Answers

With a good grasp of how coaching works, you can do a lot for yourself. At the least, you can start the process to set the stage for professional coaching to yield more substantial results.

The single most common theme that arises when I coach executives, many of whom are people of extraordinary accomplishment, is that they question their ability. That is one manifestation of their high personal goals and levels to which they feel they should and must go in performance. They are their own worst critic and end up feeding a big fear about their own competence. It's a fear that people in general don't want to disclose, but feel they must to a coach—and rightly so. I don't think there is a single person I have coached who didn't express concern about this to some degree.

Second to that concern is clarity about where they want to go. Many people succeed up to a certain level and continue to do the same stuff year after year without stepping back to analyze whether or not that course uses their time well. I challenge their habits, their superstitions, and their fears related to continuing to do things the same way. Some of these repeated actions could easily seem as silly to an outsider as the ritual some baseball players have of sitting in the dugout with their hats on inside out during a rally. Sometimes these executives will counter by saying that they want to keep on doing what they're doing—just more of it, perhaps. That's not the norm, though. A common reason executives hire a coach is because they think more of the same translates into "going nowhere."

The third issue is the path to excellence. After we discuss what they want to accomplish and go through a process of describing that as clearly as possible, we move to an analysis of where they are today, and then the third step is to establish what's missing, which leads to focus on what action they need to take to fill the holes. We identify what they need to do to make the picture whole.

You may not have access to a professional coach or may not want to take advantage of the coaches offered to you. I have had a lot of people hesitate to use inside coaches because of the confidentiality concerns related to baring their soul to someone who has coffee with their boss or, worse, with people who would like their job.

So, if you want to coach yourself:

- State where you are.
- Describe where you want to be.
- Determine the path from one to the other.
- Turn that path into an action plan.

Rock climber Stacie Blair, CEO and cofounder of the Pacific Firm, an executive recruiting company in the San Francisco Bay area, uses her sport as part of her self-coaching program. Specifically, it helps her in three primary ways: energy control, organization of thought, and problem-solving process.

It helps her counter her innate style, that is, to moderate the kind of energy that might not serve her well in the business environment. The complete physical exhaustion of a good climb helps her channel that energy. If she doesn't go climbing regularly, she says, "My brain doesn't stop chattering. I have to focus on things that take my brain 'out' and put me into a physical place where I must focus only on the next move I'm going to make. I feel as though I have to climb in my spare time to put myself at peace so I can be more productive at work."

Climbing also does not allow for panic. You have to "think your way through it. It's exactly like in business." The mechanism of dealing with a crisis moment is to sit there calmly, analyze the options, "find the right piece of gear, and move on."

As a corollary, the climbing helps her counter her innate fear that death is around the corner. You cannot panic under extreme circumstances. You have to be logical, calm, and methodical, and as a result, you don't die. That's exactly how you have to be in business, but that is not how Stacie was before she got into climbing: "From ages 29 to 35, I panicked a lot more in business."

Stacie's gut instincts about how she might train herself in the ways she needed it most were good from the start. She started climbing because she had a fear of heights, which she realized was irrational, and figured that the process of overcoming it would have all kinds of benefits. She could not have predicted that the rock climbing would give her the discipline and practice to channel her energy, stay calm, organize her thoughts, and then react methodically. As for the fear of heights, "Climbing took care of that."

Another lesson to come out of this: "In climbing, you want to lead below your skill level and follow above your skill level." The lead climber on a rock face uses holds and cracks to make progress and puts hardware, or "protection," into the rock while moving upward. The climber who follows goes along the path established by the lead climber and takes advantage of the hardware placed by the lead climber by "clipping in" along the way. Although both climbers can, at different stages, take belaying action to protect the other from falling, the person leading has a higher-risk job, so it's best to have someone there with a skill level that exceeds the job requirements.

Scuba diver and expedition sailor Cheryl Traverse, who currently heads the start-up Xceedium, also has drawn on her sports for increased self-awareness, and what that has revealed to her is a strength/weakness paradox that every other head of a start-up would do well to learn. I think of this as I read that Yahoo founder and CEO Jerry Yang planned to step down because, as *Wall Street Journal* reporter Jessica E. Vascellaro noted on November 18, 2008, "For his role in those talks [with Microsoft], Mr. Yang has been taking a beating from investors for months as concerns from inside and outside the company that he wasn't the right person to help Yahoo make painful strategic choices continued to mount."

I define the strength/weakness paradox as the premise that a positive trait, applied to the extreme, can become negative. So, if a founding CEO's success factors might be characterized as "adventurous," and "impatiently fixated on results," for example, then he might continue to rely on them as the company grows and allow them to grow into monstrous forces of decision making. The scenario seen many times is that the wunderkind then runs amok. He has no business running the company when it goes public or reaches a revenue and operational threshold that requires serious long-term planning, perseverance, and a keen sense of risk mitigation.

Cheryl knows what she likes to do and what she's good at, and her sports reinforce that self-awareness. She likes adventure and "to navigate around the existing obstacles in the marketplace. That's fairly complex, and that's the fun part of the job. I have to watch all of the market dynamics and know I can catch the wave when it comes." She likes it fast and furious. She makes the point that she is particularly good with start-ups in a fast-growth phase of development but that she may not be a good fit for larger companies because of the vision frame she has.

"If people ask me to give them my five-year plan, I say 'Forget it. There's no such thing in my business.'"

In a multibillion-dollar company, you can't give a response like that—and Cheryl is the first one to point that out. You have to have a five-year plan. It's appropriate and even desirable to have a narrow vision frame for a start-up, but when you get to a certain level of activity and revenue generation, take stock. Get the coaching you need to help expand your vision or acknowledge your limitations and either surround yourself with people who will make up for your deficits or move on.

Coaching benefits people at every level of an operation, and if you have great coaches, you can count on the fact that they have coaches too. In business there is no playbook that gives all the answers for all types of situations. Innovative thinking, bold actions, excellent timing—these are the products of human beings who keep their eyes and ears open for good ideas and reliable advice no matter what their career is.

CHAPTER 6

Give Your Head Some Air:

Liberate Your Ideas

IDEAS ZOOM AROUND your head all the time, and you may not even realize it. The input from other people, media sources, and everyday events make your synapses fire, but sometimes so fleetingly that you don't retain the thoughts they engendered. What if you overlooked the missing link in making a project succeed or, on an even grander scale, the insight leading to a new product line?

Gavin Harvey begins his day with some kind of physical activity, and when he's at home in Connecticut, it's often a ride with his favorite cycling buddy, a senior executive at Microsoft. When he's in L.A., he rides with the Griffith Park Pedalers, a group of people from television, graphic design, music, and other sectors related to the entertainment industry. As president and CEO of television network Versus (formerly the Outdoor Life Network), Gavin's head is on building this upstart sports and entertainment channel, just as he previously built the upstart E! and FX networks. As the Griffith Park Pedalers pump oxygen through their bodies, they pump ideas as well. They help each other put solutions together and put challenges into perspective. It's their clarity time.

Life hands you all kinds of useful messages, but your brain has to be trained to sort through them. A daily exercise (literally or figuratively) like Gavin's will help do that. For example, you're casually shopping for running shoes at a sporting goods store and observe an angry customer coming in with a complaint. The clerk handles it poorly. The assistant manager handles it poorly. Suddenly you see a customer who is angry not only about a defective product but also about the way the complaint about the product was handled. You think, "If they had only said x or done y, they could have turned that guy into a grateful, repeat customer." And then you get in your car and forget the whole thing.

That kind of insight might occur a dozen times a day, but if you have no effective and established way to liberate the ideas that pop into your head from time to time, all these disconnected bits of wisdom remain disconnected and largely useless.

Quang X. Pham, CEO of Lathian Health, completed his first marathon in 2008 after just three months of training.

Chapman University, 2008

Make Clarity Time a Habit

A distinguishing habit that the athlete-executives we interviewed shared is that they have certain things they do to process such ostensibly random thoughts. Being athletically inclined for the most part, a lot of them use cycling, hiking, or running as exercises for mental clarity—and they pursue the activity on a regular basis. I find that the shower is also a great place to review and assemble ideas, as are long solo hikes and a ride in the car with the radio off. The point is that these are things done regularly, not sporadically. There is a psychic connection between cycling, hiking, or taking a shower and thinking, as well as anticipation that the activity will evoke positive mental results. It is a time without distractions. The activities are not physically or mentally demanding in themselves, so energy can go into thinking. When I come back from long solo hikes on the Rocky Mountain trails near my house, I have a pocket full of note cards that I've scribbled ideas on.

Olympian Gord Woolley, founder and president of Jessam Communications, is one of many CEOs who come into the office early. But there are probably just as many who come in late and stay late. In both cases the executive uses quiet time in the office to prepare for what's next. In trying to formulate goals, visualize outcomes, explore flights of creative imagination, set priorities, examine the angles of a problem, and even write specific sentences for a memo or presentation, you must make mental space for that to happen.

For Gord, the early-morning ritual began in his bobsledding days, when the team assembled for hours of preparation. They polished the runners on the sled, walked the course, stretched, and sprinted. And then, half an hour before jumping into the sled for a run, they had quiet time.

Long before Per Welinder achieved international fame as a freestyle skateboarder, when he wanted to practice skateboarding in a parking lot, he strapped a broom to his bike along with his skateboard and hauled them both to the lot. The hour he spent sweeping the lot clean of stones so he would have a smooth practice area also allowed him time for mental preparation. When all that tidying up was done, he made magic.

Don't Let Your Work Consume You

The people featured in this book have tremendously active minds and go about life in general with an unusual intensity. Establishing "clarity time" is only one habit of their regimen in making thoughts come together and work for them. Another primary habit is doing something that actually eliminates the thinking—that is, about anything but the activity at hand.

Skateboarder Sophia Le, marketing communications manager for Kovarus, sums it up: "When I skateboard, I don't think of anything else. Even when I have a supposedly bad day skateboarding—I don't land tricks, I have a bad fall—I walk away from that experience very relieved and accomplished. There's a sense of balance in my life. I don't have to even be at the skate park. I can be on my skateboard going to the grocery store or taking a 15-minute break and skating around the parking lot, and it makes me feel reconnected to the world, to life."

What I heard time after time is "People who are intense about their work need intense distractions." The act of climbing a rock face, skydiving, or riding a bull has a cathartic effect mentally. If you dare to let thoughts of investor demands, marketing campaigns, and customer service issues intrude while you do something like that, you won't have to worry about showing up for work in the morning. When the potential consequence of performing poorly is death, you are forced to purge the mental clutter and have a laser-like focus on doing your job in the sport. Repeatedly decluttering in this manner will also help you sharpen your ability to concentrate on the grand challenges that await you at work. You become skilled at filtering out the nonessentials at any given moment.

Part of remaining sane if you are intense in your career is turning off the intensity as it pertains to work.

Mountaineering can involve expeditions of two or three months. It's hard to conceive of someone staying in touch with his office when trekking in whiteout conditions. Part of the appeal is the accomplishment, of course, but a companion to that is putting yourself in a completely different setting with a different set of challenges—even though, as we see throughout the book, the lessons learned in meeting the challenges often do apply back home.

Clearly, not everyone with that intensity wants to climb Everest or blast down a dirt road on a motorcycle every Saturday. *Intense* can take on very different appearances, but the commonality is the level of focus required to perform well in the activity. Many activities accomplish the same objective without involving anything potentially life-threatening. The activity that takes you away could be going to the theater or an art museum, lifting weights, gardening, reading a book, or spending quality time with your kids. As long as your passion for it allows you to immerse yourself in the activity, you give yourself a mental vacation.

John Wilson, president and CEO of J.C. Wilson Associates, puts concentrated energy and thought into fly-fishing; he likes the fact that he is constantly learning in doing it and never really a master at it. Others, like Kirill Tatarinov, corporate vice president of Microsoft Business Solutions, volunteer their time in an activity that consumes their energy and focus. In Kirill's case, it's teaching skiing through Outdoors for All, which provides programs for people with learning disabilities. I find that painting does the same for me. When I took a watercolor class in Yosemite, I spent two days painting waterfalls and mountains; I was totally focused on the process of painting. The rest of the world melted away.

Intense distractions are an integral part of a burn-out prevention strategy and a companion piece to activities that provide opportunity for contemplation and thought liberation.

No one with high ambitions questions the fact that there will be times when the workweek is seven days. But all of the extraordinarily successful people we talked with assert that you can't repeat that 52 weeks a year without seeing substantially diminished effectiveness. Eventually, what you accomplish in seven days could be accomplished in six days, or five, or even four. A critical success factor is incorporating activities into your life that replenish you, doing something that you can focus entirely on and leave your work behind.

Without a devotion to mental restoration and creative replenishment, you will sink into patterns that will take you from impressive to ordinary. You might still be a cut above your colleagues, but you will not be all that you could be.

Give Your Thoughts Cohesion and Power

A third component in a program of liberating your thoughts involves linking them directly to accomplishments. A well-rested mind brimming with ideas can be trained in efficiency.

Marathoner Quang X. Pham, founder and CEO of Lathian Health, handles it like this: "When I run a marathon, I've run the marathon mentally already. I see pictures of the route, the starting line.

"When I started this company, I saw myself sitting in this office. I saw myself getting the check from the VC [venture capitalist]. I saw myself presenting to big pharmaceutical executives and then convincing them to do business with me as a start-up launching a new sales channel into a very traditional, conservative industry.

"Know the enemy, know your competition, know your path, visualize it, see yourself doing what you intend to do.

"Don't just see the client; see yourself getting the order from the client."

Quang's practice has played a key role in his becoming an achiever in two highly competitive arenas: marathon running and the pharmaceutical industry.

Techniques like visualization and centering have long been in the repertoire of champions. A lot of them have arrived at the techniques by chance—maybe they have a ritual or superstition that makes them feel ready—but there are many ways to learn these techniques and use them as part of a program to achieve measurable outcomes.

As Quang suggests, the visualization begins with seeing yourself in a place and combining that with a vision of positive outcomes. Within that environment, see yourself going through each move of making a presentation, negotiating the deal, or orchestrating a board meeting. The important thing is that all you see is yourself in that setting, performing perfectly again and again.

Per Welinder takes a slightly different approach to the same exercise. Per, who earned an M.B.A. from UCLA after skyrocketing to extreme sports fame as a skateboarder, is president of Blitz Distribution. In the course of 20 years he has founded eight companies—or, as he prefers to say, brands—including Birdhouse Skateboards with longtime associate and fellow skateboard hero Tony Hawk.

During his skating days Per used visualization in a rather conventional way to rehearse his tricks mentally over and over and over again. His process: "Do it with feeling—how do I feel? Do it with time—how long will it take? Do it again until your brain completely grasps all of the elements of the journey toward success, down to the second."

Per says that visualization has also helped him "tremendously" in his business of developing brands aimed primarily at young males. But he doesn't start the process in the here and now and move forward. He first asks himself where an opportunity will thrive two or three years from now. He visualizes the success of the brand in that future. He pictures the widespread adoption of the products by the target market, and then he works backward as a way of embedding in his mind all the steps that must come first to achieve the visualized result.

Give Life to Your Ideas

When Bob Stangarone, jet pilot, got his position as vice president of corporate communications for Cessna Aircraft Company, it was like his head exploded. He knew, "This is the job I've been looking for all my life." An aviation aficionado and pilot from his youth, he suddenly had the chance to articulate his knowledge and enthusiasm on behalf of the manufacturer that has "built half the airplanes in the world," according to Bob.

I can relate to what he said because I've jumped out of many of them, including the Cessna 182, 206, and Caravan.

Working for the company became a dream come true beyond his initial expectations, which provides an important lesson about walking through the doors of companies you connect with and finding a place for yourself. It's reminiscent of great CEOs like Ira Neimark, former head of Bergdorf Goodman department store in New York, who worked himself up from doorman at the big store across the street (Bonwit Teller) to head of the finest retail establishment on Fifth Avenue. When you know what you want, you have to put yourself physically in the right place to get it.

So as a result of his position in the Cessna organization, Bob earned ratings in various types of aircraft until he qualified to fly jets. And in flying jets he fine-tuned his ability to pay attention to the details, just like in business.

In short, the more his company allowed him to learn, the better he was able to serve the company. And the more his dreams of flying were realized, the more he was able—and motivated to—liberate good ideas for the benefit of the company.

CHAPTER 7

Spawn New Tricks:

Be a Stimulus for Passion

ALTHOUGH SKATEBOARDING IS largely a solo activity, Per Welinder remembers taking breaks from his hours of solitary practice to watch his buddies skate. "There was psychological reward in seeing other people do really cool stuff," he says. Watching them inspired him to try new and different things, and they got the same boost in imagination, energy, and commitment from watching him. Sharing the passion spawned more tricks.

It doesn't really matter what the activity is that inspires passion. You want to understand the underlying reason for why you like to read books, climb mountains, or close a deal. And so, once you know that for yourself, you have a great vantage point from which to view other people's actions with the aim of understanding what kicks them into high gear.

Maybe the people in your group develop software. If the software didn't solve a problem or dramatically expand what the computer can do, would they still work those long hours? Would they care? Connect with people on their motivation for being in a particular position and you have the key to fueling their desire to be the best they can be at a job.

Carry and Spread Passion: It's a Good Virus

"A CEO has to be a cheerleader and a visionary," says skier and bobsledder Kirby Best, former president and CEO of Ingram Lightning Source, the subsidiary of Ingram Industries Inc. that provides print-on-demand services. The cheerleader molds the team together and gets everybody going in the same direction and at the same speed; the visionary determines what that direction should be.

The "cheerleader" part of effective leadership involves inspiring people with your energy. Energy in this context should not be confused with physicality, because someone like physicist Stephen Hawking can exude a contagious energy and wit even though he suffers from nearly total paralysis. It should also not be confused with a burning, aggressive intensity that people commonly find off-putting, à la Nikita Khrushchev's pounding his shoe on his desk during a debate at the United Nations.

Energy that embodies enthusiasm and commitment will affect the mindset of people around you. It's a dominant element in leading by example, which sets you up as a person with credibility and direction.

Even if you are not a manager, the approach you take to your work will impact others around you. It will either kick them up a notch in performance or drag them down. That impact can permeate your team.

Kirby and his team had trained hard for the opening of the 1981 season and expected the first race to showcase their brilliance. Although they had not even seen a sled for months, they had escalated their fitness level with sprints and weight workouts and believed that the focused cross-training would give them a solid, competitive advantage. Their goal: top third. Their result: dead last.

Chariots of Fire had just come out that first week in October 1981. It's the story of two Brits who run hard and victoriously in the 1924 Olympics, both for very different reasons but both with tremendous heart. Instead of Kirby and his team sulking at their defeat, together they discovered the movie and its inspiring theme song. They serve as each other's cheerleader. The team rallied and unanimously declared: "Let's get this fixed!" It was a turning point that took them in the direction of laughing about their arrogance in the first race and enjoying the spirit of looking forward to victories. And eventually they got them.

Help People Discover Passion Through Their Own Ideas

In going through an idea identification process to solve a problem, contributions need to be honored by the group, no matter how wacky they sound. No bad ideas. The minute someone's criticism slaps down an idea, a handful of other ideas will be suppressed.

Freestyle skateboarding pioneer and Blitz Distribution founder Per Welinder

Grant Brittain, 1988

In 1997, WatchGuard Technologies invented a new kind of Internet firewall device for small businesses and, without putting any thought into it, painted it black. This was the usual thing for engineers on a budget to do: craft their prototype product out of inexpensive black plastic and screw it together. How would they get attention for this little black box? What could they do to generate media buzz and customer enthusiasm? The young team of engineers, among whom were avowed outdoorsmen who lived in the Northwest wilderness when they could, as well as sales and marketing executives, brainstormed the problem and came up with the ideas that got them headlines: paint it red and give it a cool name. They were thinking of the well-known red fire alarms on city streets. And, because it was a firewall in a "box," they dubbed it a "Firebox." It was a victory: media pundits recognized the Firebox as something entirely new and even coined a description for it—a term still in use today: Internet security appliance.

Customers understood immediately—appliances are easy to use: just plug them in and they work—and even demonstrated some affection for the little red box that protected their networks from hackers. Three years later the company went public and the people with the wacky ideas were suddenly each worth millions of dollars and selling their red boxes worldwide. A consultant I know went to their headquarters to interview key people for a project documenting the company's meteoric rise and came away with stories of how everyone from the receptionist to the president had, at some point, contributed an idea that made a difference, whether to day-to-day operations, the products themselves, or the marketing and sales programs.

Let Quality Control Take Hold

Mountaineer Mark Richey, who is founder and head of an architectural woodworking company, admits that sometimes his team has gone to a site and been critical of their own work before the architect, owner, or general contractor has had a chance to see it or become aware of it. Everyone in the company knows the drill: fix, replace, or change the defective work without hesitation. As some people have reminded Mark, that costs money, and some others have even said to him that it's crazy to do that if no one is complaining. His counter: "I know that without question our best form of advertisement is our own work. I don't want to stand by anything that is not up to our very critical standards. That's costly, so I try to make sure it doesn't leave our shop unless it up to our standards. We have checkpoints all along the way to maintain the quality our clients demand and that we demand of ourselves." This is an ethos consistent with Alpine climbing, which is what Mark does. It is a combination of skill and confidence, and minimal hardware, in an attempt to summit a mountain with no damage to the environment and maximum focus on pure human accomplishment.

The passion is in the quality.

Live in the Future

Pilot Jeff Roberts is the group president of innovation and civil training and services at CAE. He believes that to some degree, in order to infect people with your passion, you have to live in the future. People get very enthusiastic about the future because they can make out of it what they want. It's not preordained. You can take a look at where you are today and understand how you've gotten here, but tomorrow is for you to build.

Decide where you're going to stand: in the past, the present, or the future. If you admit to being a bit of a control freak, as Jeff does, you probably will feel most comfortable standing in the future because you can have an effect on it. Jeff says, "My experience has been that if you stand in the future and can articulate the actions you need to take to create that future, people will get excited and motivated to achieve that vision."

Jeff admits that he might have an easier time than most executives in getting buy-in from his team. At CAE he is in the business of enhancing the safety and efficiency of commercial aviation. That is an easy calling to get people to rally around. Everyone can relate to raising the level of safety in flying. And efficiency is a sustainable value proposition, which in this environment translates into greater convenience and reliability for both CAE's commercial customers and, ultimately, the flying public. People at CAE get palatable satisfaction from knowing their endeavors on a particular day lead to these results. Jeff keeps their eyes on that and doesn't try to use the fees they earn from an airline as a motivating factor. It's what the job means to individual people who fly, as well as to an industry.

But no matter what business you're in, there's something at the heart of it that has to do with a calling. Businesses are created to satisfy some need, somewhere. Focus your team's attention on that core purpose to get them truly motivated, instead of hammering on the superficial motivators like increasing profit margins.

Bill Baker, polar explorer and president emeritus of Educational Broadcasting Corporation, has a main lesson that he believes got him to both the North and South Pole, as well as enabled him to launch and sustain the most watched public television station in the United States: sell the higher purpose—the greater good. That's how you get people to buy in.

Early excursions to the poles had centered on the scientific value of the explorations, whereas Bill saw a new reason to go: sharing the experience. He was on a journalistic mission to bring the poles to people who would never be able to set foot on them. He also found a way to make a difference with public broadcasting. He saw EBC as a conduit for truth, not just news.

He chose to tell people what they may not have wanted to hear but needed to hear. The focus on truth elevated the mission for people who made that experiment in television a big success.

People naturally feel more motivated to take action when they believe the desired outcome is meaningful. Whether it's an election, a war, or a business deal, if you can find a way to make that significance clear, you can infuse people around you with passion.

CHAPTER 8

Find Out What Your Gold Medal Is For:

Define Your Goals

BY THE AGE of 23, Kristen Ulmer had mastered two completely separate areas of her sport: she had earned the unofficial title of "best extreme skier in the world" and made the United States Mogul Ski Team without even having a coach.

Other people were so impressed with Kristen's abilities that they would often say to her, "Why not win a Gold Medal in the Olympics?" That kind of pressure from outside herself was inconsistent with her true motivation in the sport. She loved the movement and the radical self-expression of skiing, not the competition. To Kristen, who left the U.S. team to pursue the "extreme" style of skiing and later made the first female descent of Grand Teton, Olympic Gold was someone else's goal. She doesn't regret her decision to leave the team in the slightest.

Set Goals from the Inside

An insecure kid, when Kristen started skiing she suddenly found a confidence that began spilling over to other areas of her life—a confidence that comes from being able to make decisions consistent with internal passion rather than external pressures.

Bowing to those goals established by others and forsaking what truly drives you "will take you away from your greatest potential," she believes. "Maybe you can do it, but it will rob you of the passion." Kristen now helps people in sports and business get beyond limiting goals and find clarity about their passion in the coaching she offers through her company, Ski to Live.

In counseling senior executives in Zen wisdom, Kristen takes their focus off market dynamics and other outside factors to give due consideration to the internal component. She advises them to get in touch with their innate talents and drives so they can personally pursue excellence daily. The journey then becomes an ongoing adventure, and the personal goal evolves as excellence grows and matures.

A common scenario Kristen faces is that a client will come to her and say, "My goal is to hit the golf ball as far and as straight as I can," or "My goal is to sell more of this product than anyone else." "The analytical mind

Camille Duvall-Hero, five-time world professional slalom champion water-skier and managing director of Warburg Realty Partnership in New York
Tom King, 1993

is hard at work in those instances, figuring things out, focusing and firing on so many ideas, so quickly," Kristen says. Her coaching brings people to a different form of consciousness—one not focused on analyzing and judging, but rather on performing intuitively from memory. Some call it "the zone." It is this exercise of taking focus off the goal and putting it on the experience that, ironically, helps people achieve the goal.

Make Goals Real Through Accountability

Goal setting is a fairly academic process until you engage someone else to hold you accountable. If you come up with a set of goals and shove them into a drawer, they will probably not have the same impact as if you tell someone you trust and respect that you have specific goals and want to be held accountable for them. That's when goals have substance and gain the power of human energy and responsibility. So, while it is absolutely essential that you have clarity in your goals, it is just as essential that you declare them and be prepared for those you respect to ask you, "How close are you now?"

For many years that person in Camille Duvall-Hero's life was her father. As mentioned earlier, it was her father's initial push that got Camille into competitive waterskiing, and through her finest years in the sport she had the benefit of his engineer brain in helping her both to set goals and to achieve them. At the end of the year, Camille's father would sit down with her and her brother, also a top competitive water-skier, and discuss what happened that year and what was possible the coming year. They would write it down on a sheet of paper that they would then seal in an envelope and not look at again until the same time the next year. "You didn't have to have the list in front of you. You knew what the goals were." It was a symbolic thing, like putting them in a time capsule. They would be goals reflecting some hard metrics, like improving her slalom score by three buoys or jumping another 10 feet. She already held the world record for jumping, so exceeding that meant competing against herself. Being at the top as Camille was, many of the goals were just like that.

Now that her competitive environment is high-end residential real estate in New York, her circle of accountability partners is the 14 other top brokers at Warburg Realty Partnership and the president of the company, Fred

Peters. To stay at the top, Camille had to rethink the way she defines goals so that she could be held accountable for things she actually had some control over.

In her current world, setting goals could potentially cause huge frustration because of the vagaries of the market. They make it impossible to have anywhere near the level of control over her business that she did in waterskiing, and that is why she sets first-tier goals involving the kind of metrics over which she does have control.

Camille's primary goals are deal development activities, as opposed to variables such as transaction amounts. She focuses on the things she can do, like working hard to reinforce connections in her sphere of influence, as opposed to the results that the calls, e-mails, and showings will yield. Assuming she has a certain rate of efficiency, which she clearly does, this translates into deals at a certain transaction level.

Goals like this make it easier to adjust during a down market, she feels. She continues on the path of staying connected and growing her network while looking for different avenues to create a payoff.

When the Wall Street implosion of 2008 occurred, Camille's first thought was that it would be a bad year. Her second thought was the ways it might not be a bad year. Despite the fact that much of New York is connected directly or indirectly with Wall Street activities, she realized that "someone out there is making money" or at least not suffering as badly. So she called some of her clients and announced "opportunity time" and subsequently started showing properties nonstop. And in the real estate market, one of her "competitors" is the Internet, which savvy investors know is the source of all kinds of property records. She knew she could not cry "fire sale" if their sellers had not, indeed, dropped the price to that level.

In the midst of the crisis, something seemed to "drop out of the sky." A developer that had known Camille from her waterskiing days contacted her about an offshore property. When she heard the words "You would be the perfect salesperson for this property," she felt lucky. And then she realized the opportunity hadn't just dropped out of the sky: it was the logical outgrowth of the hard work that she had been doing and the reputation she had built. He wouldn't have called if she were just a world-class water-skier.

He had called because she stayed steady in achieving the network-related targets that ultimately ensure that a broader and broader circle of the right people know what she does and the fact that she does it well. And in a subtle way, all of those people then have a role in holding her accountable for her goals.

With a dual focus on staying true to yourself and pulling others you trust into the process of defining and pursuing goals, you are in a strong position to inspire others to support your efforts.

CHAPTER 9

Climb as Soon as the Weather Breaks:

Be Ready to Seize Opportunity

JOHN WILSON, FOUNDER and president of J.C. Wilson Associates, a San Francisco–based executive search firm, was at base camp at 19,000 feet with a friend, Louis, and a guide on Aconcagua, the Argentinean peak that is the highest mountain in the Americas. Right after dinner the weather closed in, and the wind blew all night long. He and the guide looked at each other and knew that, first thing in the morning, they would have to head down to a lower camp and then to base camp. That's what they did.

One little lesson John learned at that moment was the value of a vestibule on a tent "because we didn't have one." The vestibule allows an area for operating a climbing stove that blocks the wind; they couldn't use their stove, so they couldn't melt snow, which meant no water. Back at base camp, sitting at a comfortable 15,000 feet, they had dinner and a great bottle of Argentinean wine and thought "too bad."

The next morning a clear blue sky and almost windless day greeted them. John saw some British climbers; it was a multinational base camp. The Brits had a weather map, so he asked how the weather was looking. "Great outlook for the next few days" was their response. John went back to the tent and said, "I want to do this." So a couple of hours later they were on their way up without a guide, and two days later John and Louis summited Aconcagua.

Underlying their ability to make that summit push is something that John alludes to in talking about "hitting the reset button." After enjoying their fine Argentinean wine, he and Louis had lost a little of the emotional preparedness to go on. They had started the slide into resignation. Being able to regroup mentally to go out the next day required renewed emotional energy, and they knew it. John says they reminded each other of what a pain it would be to have to train for another attempt, fly down again, take time off from work, and other negatives that helped reignite their positive impulse to go for the summit.

Snatching victory from the jaws of defeat is possible. They seized the opportunity presented by the weather promptly and efficiently, ensuring they were ready on every level.

Break the Rules If You Want to Excel

In lots of careers, adhering to rules is required unless truly odd circumstances take hold. An air traffic controller, for example, might break the rules only if a flying saucer entered the pattern. In business, where breaking the rules generally doesn't mean someone will die, people follow rules all the time without ever considering how doing so might work to their detriment. They follow "the 22 immutable laws of marketing," "the 7 irrefutable rules of small business growth," and even "the 8 rules of business greeting card etiquette."

Lathian Health founder and marathoner Quang X. Pham offers a lesson of rebellion: play by the rules and you may not fail, but you won't excel either. By breaking a training rule for long-distance runners, he made a breakthrough in preparing for marathons. Common wisdom is that when you train for a marathon, you do only one run of 20 miles in the weeks prior, and then you taper down. He does three runs of 20-plus miles—one at 20, one at 21, and one at 22—for one primary reason: he tries to remember what his body feels like when he hits the wall at mile 18 or 19 during the training run. By repeating the experience, he can go back and figure out why he hit

Kevin Sheridan and party climbing 18,841-foot Mt. Elbrus in Russia, the highest point in Europe

the wall then and not later—what he could have done differently. He also gets practice in moving past that. So he analyzes the nature of his physical endurance and how to prolong it, as well as understanding how to activate more mental endurance. His training regimen, therefore, involves personal rules of performance enhancement. Interestingly enough, the rule-breaking program he discovered on his own is similar to the rule-breaking program used by Brazilian Ronaldo da Costa, who shattered the men's world marathon record when he ran it in 2:06:05 in the fall of 1998.

People criticizing Quang's marathon training said, "That won't work"—it did—just as the naysayers told him not to buck conventional wisdom by spending his valuable time while at the Paul Merage School of Business at University of California, Irvine, writing a "stupid business plan" and entering it in a "dumb contest." That "dumb contest" was Hummer Winblad Venture Partners' February Madness, which had been called March Madness until the NCAA said it was being fouled by copyright infringement. The contest tagline "Nothin' but the (Inter) Net" suggests the main criterion: all students submitting plans had to focus on Internet-related business ventures.

He called the business MyDrugRep.com; his plan described the world's first virtual drug representative portal. After winning the $5 million of venture capital from Hummer Winblad, he quit school and set up shop. A year later he raised another $9 million and secured an investment from Siebel systems (now part of Oracle) for software.

The summation of Quang's early rule-breaking streak in business: he had no CEO experience, no Wall Street experience, no financing experience, and only five years of working in the private sector, and within 14 months of incorporation he had raised $14 million. He followed the same clarity of vision and confidence in his skills that led him to volunteer to fly helicopter missions in Desert Shield when he didn't have the regulation number of hours in the cockpit. No matter what push-back he got, he knew he could perform. It was a decision grounded in logic, experience, self-awareness, and instinct.

Know That Maverick Thinking Does Not Mean Wacky Ideas

Combine unbridled imagination with strong powers of analysis and you get results like Ted Turner's media empire (with which he is no longer associated). An all-news network? There's not that much to report! (We know it as CNN.) A channel devoted to classic movies? People aren't going to watch recycled stuff when they can catch something new! (We know it as TCM, or Turner Classic Movies, famous for restoring and screening the best movies made.) Yachtsman extraordinaire Ted Turner's $2-billion-plus net worth proves that taking an unusual approach to a business model is not necessarily a bad idea.

When climber Stacie Blair founded the Pacific Firm, she decided to tamper with the tried-and-true model of how recruiting firms make money. She decided to charge a flat hourly rate—and still does—and led her company to status as the second-largest search and management consulting firm in the San Francisco Bay area according to the *San Francisco Business Times*.

Mountaineer Kevin Sheridan, founder and CEO of HR Solutions, began his career with a maverick idea. He spent two years raising $5 million for a concept that couldn't be tested unless the business was up and running. It was a chicken-and-egg situation. He set out to convince high school teachers across the nation that they should encourage their students to provide a spectrum of information about their academic interests and hobbies so they could be matched effectively with college recruiters. This was in the days before the World Wide Web, so the information collected in the survey would be provided as part of an electronic system, although not online. The service would be free to the students, but colleges would pay for the information, which would be closely guarded on the proprietary system. The model was that, instead of sending thousands of four-color brochures to prospective students, a university would use the database to target competitive swimmers who wanted to study journalism or students who wanted to learn specific things to go back and take the reins of a family business. *BusinessWeek* and *USA Today* featured the business called Collegiate Research Services, and more than half of all high schools in the United States agreed to participate. It might have worked if the blue chip company that provided the funding hadn't acquired a subsidiary that was in the list business—that is, a company whose bread and butter was not closely guarding information but rather selling it to anyone with pockets deep enough to afford it.

So, it didn't quite work, but Sheridan saw the power of excellent survey data, and his current company, HR Solutions International, is dramatic proof of that. HR Solutions helps organizations engage their employees and boost customer loyalty by providing results-oriented survey instruments and the follow-on training and development programs that help "Turn Data into Action™."

Like Ted Turner, Stacie Blair, and Kevin Sheridan, many other people featured in this book have had great ideas that raised eyebrows among the conservative thinkers in their industries because they were ahead of the curve. Their effort to summit, to be the fastest, to endure more than others serves as a metaphor for their vision quest in business. Entrepreneurs like these three not only saw what they could do well, and make money doing it, but also what people wanted. They had the confidence to act when they heard what the marketplace said it wanted—even when no one else may have heard that message—and the passion to back up their unconventional ideas with hard work.

Move in a Timely Manner; Opportunities Are Fleeting

In 1965, Sherman Poppen created something his wife named "Snurfer," the original of which was two skis bound together with a string allowing the rider to have a little bit of control. Twelve years later a self-described loser in shop class, Jake Burton Carpenter, created a prototype snowboard out of the Snurfer and formed Burton Snowboards. Combining his skateboarding and, to a lesser extent, his surfing experience, he had been trying to modify the Snurfer to make the device more ridable almost from the moment that Poppen introduced it to the public. When he did, he knew what he had accomplished and did not hesitate to get it in front of his target audience. Jake took a Burton snowboard to the first World Snurfer Championship in 1979 and showed his prospective customers the future of a sport called *snowboarding.* Other people had designs that played on the same concept, but it was Jake who saw the window and jumped through it fully prepared to succeed.

Recognize the Opportunity, Assemble the Team, and Take Action

In his mind, Ty Murray started earning the moniker "King of the Cowboys" went he was about eight years old, so his passion for rodeo affected many of his life choices as he grew up. Despite a set of injuries and recovery challenges, he secured his record-breaking seventh All-Around World Championship title in 1998, but in the meantime he was also a trailblazer behind the scenes. In 1992, he led the way in founding the Professional Bull Riders (PBR).

Ty doesn't try to make the history of PBR prettier than it is. He says the 20 guys who came together to form PBR "had no business experience." They were the 20 best bull riders who each invested $1,000 to kick off the venture. People laughed in their faces. "We were guys who knew how to balance a checkbook and maybe manage a single event. But, heck, we didn't rewrite the laws of physics. We just did the planning that was necessary" and combined it with the toughness and tenacity to make it work.

"We kept believing in it and kept pushing forward.

"Like I would tell kids who come to my clinics: 'You can't guarantee you're going to ride this bull. You can't guarantee that you're going to stay on. You can't guarantee you won't get hurt. You can't guarantee you're going to get a high score. The one thing you can guarantee before you crawl into the shoot is that you'll try your guts out—no matter what.'

"When you talk about how extreme sports can produce business lessons, heck, that's all we had." That is, whatever the sport had taught them was the extent of their schooling in business.

Their aim with PBR was to make bull riding "a better sport, with more people seeing it, and more money for the people doing it." Their challenge was that bull riding is a sport that very few people can relate to. They have too little exposure to it. As Ty says, "Even if you never swam competitively, you've at least been in a pool."

Ty and the original group of 20 structured their business plan around goals that made sense to their fans in an effort to expand their fan base: "We didn't reinvent anything. We just packaged it in a way that made more sense to the consumer. More fun, more followable. We wanted people to have confidence that when it was a PBR event it was the best of the best. And you could follow them in their careers." The premise was then that PBR events had the best riders on the best bulls, which can't be overlooked as a key part of competition.

Ty sees himself and the other 19 founders as coming together at the right time—acting on an opportunity presented by new television stations looking for original programming, among others—and he believes they complemented each other. Well, at least in terms of vision if not temperament. "There were times with big ups and big downs—just like riding. You learn how to keep focusing on the ups and, when you see a down, figure out how to turn it into an up." At the first board meeting there were some chairs thrown, according to Ty: "We settle things in our boardroom a little differently from most."

They settle negotiations with business partners a little differently from most too. At one meeting at the MGM Grand, where PBR was scheduled to hold finals of a competition, the two sides were at odds—$100,000 apart. Neither side was giving an inch, so Ty suggested cutting a deck of cards. He knew his audience: people in the gambling business. The MGM Grand boss thought it was a great idea. PBR won the cut.

When the PBR founders were throwing chairs at each other, CEO Randy Bernard was working out of the closet of PBR's attorney's office. Shortly afterward, the company took over the attorney's office. Then PBR took over the whole floor and finally all seven floors of the building. And then they outgrew that and built their own building. The company now has more than 100 full-time employees and more than 100 contractors.

At this point PBR claims more than 600 members in the United States and abroad, and you can see its events on NBC, Versus TV, and Telemundo. More than 600 million viewers are tuning it in, and its ratings keep rising.

As Walt Disney said, "The way to get started is to quit talking and begin doing."

CHAPTER 10

Roll with the Fall:

Practice Resilience

THE CONCEPT OF the parachute landing fall, or PLF, runs across sports. It is the maneuver you execute to avoid getting hurt, or at least to reduce body damage from a hard landing. Military parachutes and old-style sport parachutes drop the jumper in more of a straight-down manner than current parachutes, which enable skydivers to land with a forward glide (ideally). To handle the downward hit, jumpers learned to put feet together on landing and then collapse to the side on the padded parts of the body—calves, buttocks, and then shoulders—dissipating the force and minimizing the chance of breaking anything while still protecting the head. A person who has done a good PLF ends up in a body position that looks like a banana. Depending on the sport, an analogous fall might also involve a roll on a mat, over handlebars, on a ski slope, or down a vert ramp.

When you see it, you know the person knows what she's doing. She is up to the current challenge and probably ready for more.

Skier Julie Pearl, founder of Pearl Law Group, the largest woman-owned law firm in the San Francisco Bay area, says that, when she saw her daughter fall off her bike and roll well, she and her other kids applauded. That's because she sees "rolling with the fall" as fundamental to success.

Julie builds on a quote from Pulitzer Prize–winning author Pearl S. Buck in explaining her belief to her staff: "Every great mistake has a halfway

Sophia Le, marketing communications
manager for Kovarus
Lauren Williams, 2008

moment, a split second when it can be recalled and perhaps remedied." Julie explains,

"With mogul skiing, you're not always able to see ahead of you, so you need to trust your ability to fall well. That halfway moment is aligning your body right as you are up in the air, about to crash down. You have a split second in which you can align your body to fall on the side, align your legs without breaking them, and so on. People make mistakes all the time by not taking that split second and realigning, thereby turning a potential disaster into a minor inconvenience."

A lot of things in business happen like that. When things go awry, Julie pulls her team together to figure out what the quick fix was, is, or could be. What does the protective fall look like in this context? What would you do next time to make "the fall" even better? The exercise helps them keep their focus, stay calm, and redirect their energy from fear damage to a renewed sense of competence.

Exploit Setbacks for the Lessons They Provide

World-class mountaineer Chris Warner cites failures, in the technical sense, as some of his greatest achievements. Failure to summit one mountain on a particular day yields the tactical information to summit the world's most difficult mountain the following year. Failures provide prime opportunities to learn as long as you do a logical debriefing on them in a nonaccusatory way.

Olympian bobsledder Gord Woolley's guidelines on innovation tell you how to move from failure to stardom in six steps:

1. Admit the error.
2. Learn from the failure.
3. Assess and analyze what went wrong.
4. Make sure you don't repeat the mistake.
5. Fix whatever went wrong and do it without blame.
6. Redouble your efforts to get it right the next time.

This exercise has absolutely nothing to do with pointing fingers. It is about taking actions toward a desired outcome. When uncontrollable circumstances are the critical factors in the failure—like the corporate equivalent of whiteouts or avalanche conditions—the analysis automatically maintains a humane and civil tone. But when the critical factor is someone's not having the physical or mental conditioning to go on, the only way to benefit from the experience is for the analysis to remain an exercise of the brain and not the hormones. Everyone knows you didn't succeed, so figure out how to make this situation better instead of spanking the guy who couldn't keep up.

Learn. Minimize the chances that this will happen again. Send the message that this wasn't the desired outcome but there will be times when not getting the desired outcome yields huge insights about avoiding future traps and even surpassing your performance expectations.

As Gord described in his checklist, failure fuels innovation. It can inspire gold medal performance. A classic example is how Tony Hawk approached the trick of his life.

Early in his career, Tony always had the same stress feelings that scrambled his energy at the X Games. Tricks he knew he could do blindfolded in practice took him down in competition. He'd compete. He'd fall. Eventually, he fell less and less and a legend was born.

Tony swallowed a big loss when he came in third at the summer 1998 X Games in San Diego, his hometown. He'd already won 12 world championships, so placing third increased the pressure on him to come up with an unprecedented feat to redeem himself. His next event, at the Münster World Championships in Germany, seemed jinxed from the start. First he had to take a late plane that put him into Germany the night before the qualifying runs. Then the airline lost his luggage—he had a board but no clothes. He had to borrow gear for practice the next morning. When his gear arrived, he had to hurry back to the hotel and then return to the park to qualify. In spite of it all, he qualified first: "Everything felt right."

Everything kept feeling right. It was a different country, a different contest, and a very different stress level.

"It was more relaxed than at the X Games. There were four runs. My first run, I was fairly conservative, but I did things that I knew would be a little bit harder. A little bit risky, but not too much. The next time, I upped the ante. On the third run I pretty much tried whatever I could because judging was based on only the best run out of the four. I felt like I'd already put together my best run, so on the third I just took all the risks and pulled it off."

He threw in a 720 (double spin), varial 540 (the skater does one and a half spins and spins the board a half), and a front-side caballerial (a no-hands 360, with the skater blind to the ramp at the start of the rotation). It's a trick more commonly seen in a movie, where the skater gets several takes. A lot of the other tricks Tony added to his 45-second run were the same level of difficulty—"tricks I generally wouldn't try in a contest, but I felt it was the right time."

He won, but that isn't what made Münster 1998 a high point. It was because he skated with heart, reaching a performance level that he found exhilarating.

"When I won, I was elated because of my skating. Even if someone else had put something together that the judges decided was a winning run, it wouldn't really have detracted from how I was feeling just from having skated that well. For me, it was just about giving my personal best, and it doesn't matter how I've ended up in the rankings if I've skated my best."

Do not cue the heartening music at the end of the movie quite yet. At the X Games the following year, Tony had bigger plans than just winning. His "failure" in 1998 would sink into oblivion if he pulled off what he planned that year.

In the best trick contest, he went for a 900, or two and a half rotations. It's a trick in which the skater spins hard and has to land at the right angle or he will feel like he was in a car wreck. Tony knew that well, because he'd knocked himself out trying to pull it off for 10 years. Incrementally, he kept learning from his failure. His experience at the Münster World Championships also reinforced what he knew about overcoming both a sense of failure and lousy odds: you have to go all out—with heart. When he nailed the 900, the crowd shrieked and stormed the vert ramp to adore the god of skateboarding. The feat is still a record.

Tony failed for 10 years, and even 10 times in one night, before the headlines blared: 1-900-HISTORY.

There are countless examples of the business version of this. Skateboarder Sophia Le, who is the marketing communications manager for Kovarus, bridges the sports and business lesson in this way: "You can be skating alone, in total control in open space, and all of a sudden you hit something, and you go flying. You look down and you don't see a stick or a divot or anything. A tiny pebble can throw you off balance on your board, and you are suddenly on the ground." (I refer you to Chapter 6, because former professional skateboarder and now clothing mogul Per Welinder talks about hauling a broom to the parking lot and sweeping for an hour before he practiced his freestyle routines.)

"What I learned is that it's kind of funny, and you have to roll with it —literally," Sophia says. "You laugh at yourself. Pick yourself up. And you get back on your skateboard." There are times at work when you're not in control of the situation, and that certainly doesn't make you look so good. Something shows up unexpectedly and throws you. You don't look so good at the moment, but you can't let it get to you. Her message to herself is "Get back on that board."

A specific business example that reflects the same kind of dogged hard work and quantifiable success comes from Deidre Paknad at PSS Systems. She wants customers to be "crazy in love" with her products, but even with that level of commitment, she admits, things don't always go well.

The aftermath of disappointment will either yield a stronger relationship with the customer or lead to dissolution of it. One of Deidre's customers had product failures that put its business at risk just before the July 4 holiday—and the problems could be claimed by both the customer and Deidre's company. Rather than just fixing her part and taking a few days off, Deidre committed her engineering resources and personal involvement for a 10-day period over the holiday to help the customer correct the problems—on her side and theirs. The errors on both sides were corrected, and the systems on both sides improved. No one had to lose, and no one did. "The payback of what came out of that crisis is about 10 references a week and four published presentations by that customer at large conferences, where they told everybody in the room that we are the absolute best partner." Did she ever think during that 10-day period that they were spending too much money and human resources on the problem? Without hesitation, she says no.

Deidre made history, with a capital *H*, in the mind of the customer—and where else does it really matter? That's a win that prompts a celebration by the team and the fans.

Analyze Setbacks So You Head Straight to Success Instead of Repeating Mistakes

"King of the Cowboys" and Professional Bull Riders president Ty Murray breezed through his first six championships in six years. His goal was breaking the record of six championships, so the adrenaline was high. He was almost home. And then came the knee injury, the first serious body malfunction that took him out of competition for three years.

Ty had ridden every day since he was a teenager, but the badly damaged knee required reconstructive surgery and a nine-month rehabilitation period. "I had the surgery and was insane on the rehab: six days a week, two hours a day." He even had both knees done at the same time to take care of an old injury on the other knee. He figured if he'd be out nine months anyway, he might as well make everything right.

Ty came back with his knees stronger than they had ever been, and he retrained his brain to recognize this accomplishment. Never, for a moment, did he want to be that guy who doesn't hurt anymore but keeps on limping out of habit, not necessity.

With that kick-butt attitude, he returned to rodeo—for a little while anyway. As soon as he went back, he dislocated a shoulder. Staying out for an entire year without riding had corrupted his muscle memory. In the months he had trained to become the Bionic Man from the knees down, he didn't realize how out of focus the rest of his body was for riding. So the next round of rehab put that shoulder into the best shape it had ever been in—and then he promptly dislocated the other shoulder.

After that Ty trained everything. He dramatically escalated his overall fitness with a commitment to martial arts training. Finally his whole body was in the best shape it had ever been in. No part of him went untrained. "I was doing 2,000 push-ups a day and could have done 4,000," he says. Core strength was of consummate importance.

After having prizes come naturally year after year, Ty had to plan meticulously for success and aggressively train his way back to excellence. Riding had always come naturally before because his body was accustomed to it. Until he suffered that series of injuries, he didn't realize all of the component parts of what he did: "I had never even been off for two weeks before, let alone three years."

The first knee surgery occurred in 1995. He won his seventh, and the all-time record-breaking, championship in 1998.

How did that experience help him in business? Ty says, "I learned to step back and redefine the problem." In the case of bull riding, the problem was that fans had a hard time following the sport; PBR decided to break with a tradition of randomness and institute a point system to clarify who the competitors are and how they rank. Ty and his fellow cowboy-businessmen in PBR saw NASCAR as a model of how to build momentum week after week. They succeeded by putting great riders on great livestock in a series of competitions that is now televised.

Let the Pain of Failure Help You Set Priorities

"On Aconcagua, at about 23,000 feet, I would take three full breaths and one step, and then every once in a while I'd decide to pick up the pace, so I'd take two breaths and then a step. My heart would race up to 140 beats a minute, and I'd start to black out."

Aconcagua was one of the mountains that nearly broke mountaineer Guy Downing, former Wall Street investment banker and founder and managing director of Columbia West Capital: "I came close to saying 'I can't do this anymore.'" He describes his source of renewed energy and commitment exactly the same way that John Wilson did when he and his climbing partner changed their minds about making another summit attempt on the same Argentinean giant: it took so much work to get there that he really didn't want to have to go through all that effort and expense again (see Chapter 9).

Guy summarizes the thought that drove him on like this: "When I've invested so much to get from there to here, there's no way I want to come back and have to spend 18 days of work to get to where I am today. I have to find the strength to get this done now." He describes the alternative—that is, coming back another time—as "unbearable."

Honoring your passion and achieving your goals sometimes takes more than acting on the power of positive thinking. The power of negative thinking, in the sense that Guy captured it, draws on a primal urge to avoid the greater pain. In his mind, the logic that drove him upward when quitting seemed so reasonable was that the pain of continuing would be nothing compared to the pain of having to come back and start all over again.

In joining an international expedition of skydivers to jump onto the North Pole, I had prepared my mind and my gear and then flew to Russia. The aircraft that carried us to the North Pole was an Ilyushin 76, a four-engine Russian military jet transport. The plan involved teams of 10 skydivers leaving the aircraft simultaneously so that we would land close together. That was one of many ways we hoped to mitigate the danger of the jump: we would be there for one another in case of a bad landing and there for one another if we landed well but away from any other support.

We did an altimeter calibration pass at 1,000 feet so that all of the skydivers on the plane could adjust our altimeters and automatic activating devices (AAD). The AAD fires the reserve parachute if the main parachute has not been deployed by a particular, preset altitude.

The plane climbed much more rapidly than had been planned to our exit altitude of 10,000 feet. This aircraft had only so much range, and the pilots felt they had to take action quickly so they could get back to the base at Khatanga Airport in Siberia more than 1,000 miles away. We had been told that there would be about 10 minutes between altimeter calibration and exit. Instead it was two or three.

Suddenly the exit light and horn in the aircraft went off—screaming mechanical devices that insisted, "Get out!" We scrambled to the door. With the plane going 170 miles an hour, we had to exit on cue or we would bypass our target. Since the North Pole is not a landmass, but rather floating ice sheets, missing the target potentially equated with disaster. We also had to exit on cue as a team; the speed of the aircraft meant that we had to exit together if we were going to land together.

The drone of the plane made talking a near impossibility, and the substantial polar suits we wore covered our heads and mouths, as well as our bodies, so communication among team members came down to a nod or a head tilt. The suits also disrupted our orientation with our own skydiving gear.

Suddenly I was over the North Pole, about to exit the aircraft at 10,000 feet with my nine teammates, and I realized I had not tightened my leg straps. Due to the bulk of the Arctic gear, I hadn't realized that I had made this potentially fatal mistake. The loose leg straps would result in my harness shifting upward, with my chest strap slamming up across my face and probably knocking off my goggles. At the temperatures we faced in free fall over the pole, a single tear and blink of an eye would freeze my eyelashes together. If that occurred, even if I could deploy my parachute, I wouldn't be able to tell if I were heading for ice or water. The worst-case scenario would be that the chest strap would shift above my head and I would no longer be in the harness. I would pitch forward and continue in free fall for what would be my last skydive.

I had a moment to tighten my leg straps and make a decision about whether or not to keep going. Outside that airplane loomed an extraordinary and extreme environment I'd never been in before. I did not want to miss it, and while I had tightened my leg straps, there was a distinct possibility that I had neglected other last-minute checks and elements of preparation that were critical to my safety and survival because of the rushed exit.

In retrospect, I realized that I left the plane because the pain of going back home without having exploited this once-in-a-lifetime opportunity surpassed the pain of wondering whether or not I had done everything to do a safe skydive. Maybe I would have made a different decision at that moment if I had not bypassed a few prime opportunities before; I did not want my trip to the North Pole to symbolize my inability to take action and become a recurring regret. I suffered that greater pain of not taking advantage of a rare opportunity before and learned that it is, indeed, a greater pain than taking an intelligent and worthwhile risk. My mind zipped through the preparations I'd made to mitigate the risk of the North Pole jump, including jumping with the same gear while wearing the polar suit and goggles. I concluded that my awareness of the loose leg straps was more a sign of my overall preparedness than a sign of other potential dangers.

Just as it did for me at that moment above the North Pole, the pain of not moving forward on Aconcagua had multiple facets for Guy. There was the pain of disappointing himself by turning back. There was the pain of disappointing the people back home who had supported him emotionally. And then there was the supreme pain: disappointing the people who were with him on the climb.

He knew, "When you hit the wall and you have to cash it in, you jeopardize everyone else's chance of going on." They would have to pull a guide at the very least, and it might even cause the expedition leader to call off the entire summit attempt.

A lot of that emphasis on team dynamic affects his investment banking business, even more than it ever affected his operations as a Wall Street banker in a 10,000-person company. His success with Columbia West Capital means having a team that functions, at least with a subliminal sense, that the supreme pain is disappointing the other people who are on the climb:

"For me, starting Columbia West as an entrepreneur, founder, and leader, there definitely is a similar sense of responsibility to the team as there is on the mountain. The same dynamic can exist, I suppose, at a larger organization, but at CWC the sense of obligation is much more real and tangible. We had employees that left stable jobs to come join us as a start-up, believing we could 'make it to the summit.' That was a risky proposition for them and took a leap of faith in the team we had assembled. While not life or death as it can be in the mountains, it is still your livelihood and family financial security at risk.

"I suppose, in a sense, in this world I am the 'mountain guide.' On the mountain I am part of a team, looking to the leadership and experience of the guides for our success and safety, as well as our fellow expedition team members. At CWC, I have the same responsibility to the team, but both as expedition member and one of the expedition leaders with my partners."

———

Every one of the athlete-executives we talked with had faced pride-squashing setbacks at some point, and every one of them used and built on the lessons of the experience rather than let it narrow their possibilities in the future.

CHAPTER 11

Stretch If You're Too Short:

Never Give Up

WHEN ACCOMPLISHING SOMETHING in particular holds extreme importance for you, you will do what it takes to get the job done. A goal consistent with your passion provides both the foundation and the direction for that level of persistence.

On the other hand, if you don't care that much about the task at hand, you don't feel any pain when the job falls off your radar. The mantra "Never give up," therefore, has real relevance only if you honor your passion.

Kirby Best, former CEO of Ingram Lightning Source, says he's not a natural athlete and too short for some of the sports he's done. Nevertheless, he has competed internationally in 10 sports: gymnastics, rugby, rowing, downhill racing, freestyle skiing, speed skiing, biathlon (cross-country and rifle shooting), bobsledding, mountain biking, and polo. His most notable achievements were as part of the Canadian ski and bobsled teams. Kirby's brother called him an "illiterate George Plimpton," the journalist famous for competing in professional sports events and then documenting his experiences in books and articles for *Sports Illustrated*.

For years and years, athletics called to him: "My goal was to do as well as I possibly could in as many sports as I possibly could."

Even though he always liked sports and had a fierce competitive streak, Kirby did have a turning point that reinforced an innate tendency never to give up. "What really changed my life was getting involved in the rowing program at school," he says. All through practice he held his own in the eight-man shell. At five-foot-seven—short for a rower—he had a hard time doing what was required: "I learned that the sweep of the oar depended on how far you could reach your arms back and forth." By extending his knuckles straight and relying on his fingertips, he could get an extra inch and a half; with the sweep of a 10-foot blade, that translated into an extra foot at the far end. By doing that he was able to simulate being a much taller person. After he had won a number of prestigious competitions early on, some of his teammates went on to win gold at the 1984 Olympics in Los Angeles.

Live the Belief That Packing It In Is Not an Option

Endurance athletes like Sharon Kovar, who runs extreme races that may exceed 100 miles as well as races that are as "short" as a half marathon with a high degree of difficulty, know that sometimes the only option is to finish what you start. Going into a race, Sharon is well aware that she'll still be running long after her family and friends who waved to her at the starting line have moved on to lunch and dinner. And it's the same thing with mountaineer-executives who tell us about putting one foot in front of the other for days, or even weeks, at a time as they move toward the summit of Everest or K2.

In any situation that tests your endurance, whether it's sport or business, the pain and exhilaration of the challenge may take turns dominating your thoughts, but as long as you have a passion for what you're doing, the exhilaration will win. At the very least, you will periodically breathe a sigh of gratitude that you are still moving forward and find the exhilaration a bit farther down the road.

Know That You May Need to Revise Your Goals and Methods to Keep Moving Forward

Without goals you will have random movement in no particular direction. The question you have to ask on a regular basis is "How are we moving closer to our goals?" Having clarity of goals gives you the criteria to determine whether you're making progress.

Linear forward movement is not always making progress, however. You might need to revise your model for moving toward the goal. Skier and Microsoft executive Kirill Tatarinov says, "The actual shortest line is not necessarily the straightest line, in skiing or in business. Sometimes if you take the straightest line, you fall. You need to be able to look ahead and draw your coordinates to get where you want to go."

When I'm hiking in the Rockies, I look at the summit of a nice little 13,000- or 14,000-foot peak and know that I would exhaust myself—not to mention violate fundamental National Park rules—if I didn't use the switchbacks to get there. These zigzag trails put all human traffic on a path that winds upward in a way that works

Sharon Kovar, former manager of succession planning and development for Chevron, competing in an ultramarathon in Namibia

with the contours of the mountain, not against them. There are other, profound reasons for not stomping or crawling straight up a cliff, though.

Alpine climber Mark Richey and founder of Mark Richey Woodworking says that the compelling reason for sometimes taking a less direct route is not just a practical decision but an artful one: "For me climbing is as much about the style and approach as it is about the final outcome." He has chosen to stay true to the Alpine style rather than drive hardware into the side of mountains. He chooses a no-impact approach to reaching the highest point that has resulted in about 25 new routes up some of the world's most daunting rock faces.

A person like Mark becomes an artist when he is not necessarily interested in the simplest or easiest route. He is interested in the artful route that reflects his values.

Sometimes you may even need to alter the goal itself. Just because a goal is valid when a project starts doesn't mean it will be permanently valid. You don't want to change your goals five times a day like someone with attention deficit issues. You do want to know that the goals you established up front will make sense.

Changes in resources, market conditions, and the competitive environment will be the three primary external reasons why your goal must change. Those changes could dictate that you need a more ambitious goal or that you need to scale it back. Act agilely when the evidence is in, but don't stop dead in your tracks. If you need to get to market sooner, or can wait to get to market later, do not irrationally cling to your original plan.

Stay open to unexpected outcomes and rewards—they may be better than your original goals.

A change in passion will be the primary internal reason why you must change your goal. The concept "Never give up" remains valid only as long as the goal you're never giving up on makes sense for you. As part of his journey toward pioneering reality TV, Mark Burnett, now known for enduring hits like "Survivor" and "The Apprentice," completed two Raid Gauloises. Until Mark's own adventure race called Eco-Challenge entered the picture in 1995, the Raid had the reputation as the toughest race on earth. Competitors trekked, climbed, kayaked, and engaged in whatever athletic activity was required by the environment and race organizers to go from the starting point to the finish line, which they would see after 10 days if they were tough enough. A little heady from leading the first American teams ever to finish the Raid, Mark committed to a third one despite the fact that his head and passion centered on launching Eco-Challenge. Even as teams checked gear and took positions to start the 1994 Raid, Mark was recruiting them for his race. That year, Team America Pride began their trek with a humiliating navigational error that cost them 24 hours. They found their way and pushed on. One team member wrenched his knee badly and had to drop out. The rest pushed on. Discord among them compounded relentless physical discomfort. They pushed on. The whole time, Mark had a "Never give up" attitude, just as he had before; the problem was, this time it was completely misplaced. As he says in his 2005 book, *Jump In*, "My focus should have been wholly on preparing to produce Eco-Challenge. Eco was my future and my passion." The team dropped out of the race, and at first the concept of quitting felt like a horrible rash. But Mark's common sense kicked in and taught him lessons that have helped him reach unprecedented goals in television. Among them is that you should apply "Never give up" to the goal that is your passion. If you've made the mistake of taking on too many challenges at one time, get your priorities clear in your head and put your energy into the truly important ones.

Chart Your Progress

For lengthy or complex projects, you need an effective way to determine whether you are making progress because the goal will not be achieved for a while. It is preferable for the interim steps to be defined quantitatively, but your qualitative assessments of progress will ultimately yield some kind of metrics. For example, a campaign to establish public acceptance of a new product may begin with media coverage, move to advertising, and then involve product placement in high-visibility arenas like TV shows and sporting events. By their nature those activities cannot necessarily be evaluated in terms of "how many" and still have meaning. There is a level of subjectivity in determining the amount of progress. It is likely, although not guaranteed, that a single positive mention on "The Oprah Winfrey Show" could turn a new consumer product into an overnight sensation. It is likely that 200 mentions in small-town papers and selected websites would not mean as much, but then viral marketing might come into play and make those hits exponentially more valuable. At some point in the campaign, though, you have to get quantitative—you have to start measuring the success of such efforts in terms of sales and market share.

Sometimes executives try too hard to quantify things to the extent that the measurement has a negative impact instead of serving as an impetus to progress and greater achievement. Focus on the funnel effect drives them to ask for a certain number of weekly cold calls or presentations. That's valid to the extent that it does more than generate a flurry of Friday afternoon calls to people who are weak prospects. A focus on the single, high-impact action is valid, too, but does not fit easily into an evaluation system based on metrics.

The best sales incentive programs are focused more on results than on methods. The use of excessive metrics tends to be the refuge of people who are still developing their management talents.

It's also true that some people will make the argument that they are after the "big hit" as a way of getting out from under the burden of doing cold calls, for example. But your assessment of the person's track record, reporting, knowledge of the so-called big hit, and other factors should give you the foundation for deciding whether the assertion merits a get-out-of-jail-free pass on the qualitative evaluation. This is one example of how management takes shape as an art and not a science. In her position as director of development at a museum, my friend Mary was once given an employee to supervise who was wildly independent and creative in his fund-raising. Logic told her he probably wouldn't provide weekly written reports, so she said simply, "Just tell me at the end of the week how much money you've raised, and I'll put it in my report." They had no trouble working together successfully. Her bigger challenge was convincing her boss that the scanty reporting was an investment in her colleague's productivity.

Fixate on Results

Goal clarity relies on a clear sense of priorities, and generally some of them are stated while others are implied.

A goal like "I will summit Everest" involves a tangible result. It's something that either happens or doesn't happen; it can be determined by measurements and documented by photographs. The goal you may not state, which is arguably more important, is that you will also return in a reasonably healthy state from Everest. Another one is that you will do whatever you can to protect and assist your fellow climbers.

Your stated goals for your company may be setting records for quarterly profits and increasing market share by 10 percent. If you have no implied goals about how you do it, then fixating on results involves pursuing those successes at any cost. You wouldn't give consideration to other priorities, which could include brand building and customer retention, for example.

Fixating on results serves you well when you know both the stated and the implied goal, that is, when your priorities truly guide the decisions you make in pursuit of the goals. This is the path to fixating on a goal without having tunnel vision about it. While the differentiation gets more play in Chapter 22, I will say here that you have peripheral vision for a reason and it is a physiological metaphor for what you need as an executive. The mountaineers we interviewed all spoke about the constantly changing circumstances on a mountain. The goal of summiting never changed. The focus on the goal never changed. But the decisions along the way may have involved making route changes, leaving certain gear behind, and adjusting the timing of a summit attempt. Fixation on the goal without regard for time of day and weather—that is, tunnel vision about the goal—spells disaster for someone at a very high elevation. Jon Krakauer's description of the disastrous Everest summit in his book *Into Thin Air* captures the idiocy of that corrupted goal fixation.

You may achieve your goal if you tune out input that gives you a broad and balanced perspective of the challenge, but you may not survive the effort. Be uncompromising in making decisions that enable you to achieve your goal while honoring your true priorities.

CHAPTER 12

Think like a Pilot:

Focus Yields Efficiency

"One of the philosophies we put in place at CAE is that one of the first things you have to do is think. Flying is a thinking game. Business is a thinking game. Once you've thought through things, you have to prioritize. These are the things that are most important, and these are the actions I need to take. And then you have to focus. Once you focus, you can act."

—Pilot and certified instructor Jeff Roberts, group president, civil training and services and innovation, CAE Inc.

THIS BOOK PRESENTS many interrelated concepts, but three in particular address how you personally handle goals. One is your clarity about a goal. Another is your dogged persistence in achieving it. The third is your adaptability in adjusting course as you move toward it. All three of them involve putting thought into things that could occur in the future. All three of them involve being prepared so that if something unanticipated occurs you will be ready to deal with it, having walked through all possibilities in advance rather than trying to tackle a problem for the first time once your stress level has already gone up.

Credit Suisse's equity trading desk lead Parks Strobridge competing in an Ironman qualifying triathlon at Lake Placid, New York

Action Sports International

You can't do any of this without focus.

Focus at the Right Level

Just as pilots like Jeff Roberts will sometimes fly high with the jets and other times low to the ground with the crop dusters, you have to adjust your focus for the task at hand.

Think of flying at 40,000 feet as being in a strategic, big-picture mode. Being in a tactical and implementation mode is like flying close to the dirt. You need to be able to do both. Part of prevailing in a given situation means knowing what flight altitude will help you effectively address your current challenge. Understand the broad context into which your challenge fits—the big picture—but know when you need to get intimate with the details of a situation. Just as you cannot discern the detail on the ground from 40,000 feet, there will be times when you need to dive down for a close look. You'll be flying low. Maybe even, as the military pilots put it, following the map of the earth.

Cheryl Traverse, president and CEO of Xceedium, uses scuba diving and expedition sailing metaphors to illustrate this and feels that these activities are essential in helping her do her job of providing vision and direction for the company: "It is the job of the CEO to have the 40,000-foot perspective." This is Cheryl's sixth successful start-up, so she has the street credentials to say what works.

The process of adjusting focus begins with her getting the view from above so that the details in the picture make sense when she drops down from the strategic to the tactical level.

At the phase Xceedium had entered when I talked with Cheryl, her strategic aims centered on channel development. At the end of the quarter, the big question was how many partners there were that generated revenue.

"That's the net net," she says. "It's not about signing up the partners, training classes, or the number of deals they have in your pipeline. It's how many deals closed." Seeing the landscape of the total number of deals and the source of those deals is the 40,000-foot view. That high-level outlook will also give you a strong sense of how much revenue is currently generated through the channels. Then all the details fall into place in the picture. If you were planning to have 10 percent of your revenue come through channels in a particular quarter, and that did not happen, then having the benefit of the high view, you can drop down and get your nose in the details and they will have meaning about why the target was not met.

"If you don't think at the 40,000-foot level, none of the details will mean anything to you."

But even a CEO doesn't fly at 40,000 feet all the time. Cheryl believes, "If you don't do it 25 percent of the time, you're not going to succeed. That's the percentage of thinking devoted to vision and strategy, and then 75 on the tactics."

One of the times to go into the low-to-the-ground, tactical thinking is when events or plans need analysis from the "bottom up." For example, if her vice president of sales says that he will deliver 80 percent of the revenue through channels the following year, she will take the person through the process of checking tactics. She already has the top-down view firmly in her head, and with him she will review the bottom-up perspective.

At the end of the month the percentages reverse, because Cheryl goes back into high-altitude mode for her board meetings. Her board wanted to meet every six weeks, and she said no. She wanted to be sure that every month she forced herself to focus exclusively on the big picture. She uses it as a way to keep herself strategically alert.

Exercise Focus to Support Discipline and Time Management

Triathlete Parks Strobridge runs Credit Suisse's equity trading desk. The activity and pressure to perform remain constant. The big variable is going from intense to more intense. Parks sees his preparation for competing well in each of the three athletic challenges of triathlon—swimming, biking, and running—as forcing him to have a sense of schedule structure, time management, and efficiency of operations. He brings all that to work with him so that when intense goes to more intense he has a grasp of benchmarks and is geared up to reach the finish line.

Distinguish between activity and progress in your work, as the finest athletes do in their sports. Once you know the basics of rock climbing, you can work your way up a familiar route again and again by grabbing handholds and jamming your hands into cracks that you know are there.

You can maintain fitness for the sport by doing that, but you don't raise your skill level. There's no question about the fact that you need the foundation skills to do more than repeat a success; those foundation skills give you certain efficiencies in movement. To progress beyond that, however, requires more than muscle memory: you have to think.

Focus, in the way pilot Jeff Roberts talks about it, is a cognitive process that puts your basic skills to work in an organized fashion. It is thinking with your mind centered on the steps toward achieving a goal.

Having absolute clarity about what you want to achieve is essential to seeing the path toward it. Think of the last time you had a specific project to do by a specific deadline. Let's say you had to prepare a 20-minute presentation on plans for the next quarter to your senior management team and you had four days in which to prepare it. There was an absolute, known outcome guiding your work, and keeping your eyes on that made you efficient, or at the very least improved your efficiency. Part of what helped that occur was your goal clarity, and part of it was the need to make a solid presentation. You knew the alternative would stink.

When the goal seems huge and amorphous, it's much harder to get yourself, much less anyone else around you, into high gear and driving straight for the end point. You can have a goal like that, but you need to break it down so that you can focus on the clear benchmarks and on the deadlines on the way to the final deadline.

When Maryann gets a contract to write a book, she knows the ultimate goal is not just words on page. It's a two-fold goal of creating a book that serves an informational need and making sure that consumers who need and want that information know about the book. But first, she has to write it, so finishing the manuscript becomes the first tangible goal. From that point she back-plans. That is, beginning with the due date for the manuscript, she works backward to create a series of no-later-than deadlines. By z date, a word count of 50,000 must be reached. By y date, all photos must be in hand. By x date, all interviews must be completed. By mentally organizing her process in that manner, she actually knows the answer when someone asks, "How's it going?" And when a coauthor or someone gathering research asks, "What can I do now to contribute?" she knows what to say.

As an example, let's say your big, amorphous goal is increasing market share. With her 40,000-foot view of the possibilities, your CEO has declared that the company now has 23 percent market share and she wants to see 28 percent market share by the end of the year. How are you going to get that additional 5 percent? You look at your options: Revise distribution channels. Revisit pricing policy. Acquire the competition to buy market share. Introduce a new product. You can go on and on, trying to fly high so you can see the landscape of routes to success. You decide which paths are valid and turn them into priorities. Then you organize those priorities by order of importance and when they need to occur.

Use Your Focus to Help Structure Priorities and an Action Plan

Your focus leads to your own efficiency in the way you structure your work process and your time. It also leads to the efficiency of other people around you, who, through your leadership and action, experience the difference between activity and progress.

At that point the number of units going out the door takes on significance for everyone that is greater than "good numbers." They are numbers in relation to a goal; they represent quantifiable progress toward increasing market share. They represent a step on the path.

Focus is not just an organizational practice, therefore. It is a cognitive exercise aimed at progress toward a goal.

Versus TV head Gavin Harvey has specific ways of boosting his ability to focus. One involves getting the oxygen pumping through his body, another is a way to eliminate extraneous thoughts, and the third is toning his focus by forcing himself to sustain it.

First, he kicks his morning off with a great physical activity, usually riding his bike with friends and colleagues, because he feels it empowers him throughout the day. To reap maximum benefits from this, though, he does not waste time with last-minute preparation. He organizes his clothes, his bike, his water, and everything else he'll need for the ride the night before so he can charge out the door. "When it's time to execute, I want to be ready to go," he says.

Second, he hits the open road with his motorcycle. Gavin sees motorcycling as "meditative in an adrenaline-charged kind of way." It serves a function in his life that's complementary to what he gets from the cycling: "It's all about risk management. When you get on a motorcycle, it's all about preparation—know where I'm going, know the tires are pressurized correctly, know the weather, road conditions—and decluttering. If a thought about your family or business intervenes, you could be risking your life. It requires 100 percent concentration on the task at hand." He says that the parallel to business is that when a challenge faces you, such as a down economy that requires you to revamp a budget at the last minute, you must have all cylinders firing for as long as it takes to do the job well. It requires the ability to declutter. You have to "focus ruthlessly" to get everything out of your mind so you can reach the goal.

Third, he allows fly-fishing to teach him how to sustain focus: "I am impatient with myself. I can't believe I've been trying to learn fly-fishing for two years, and I can't tell you how many times just this year I've hit myself in the back with my fly. I have to have my fishing buddy pull the fly out of my leg." But Gavin has grown to appreciate this thing that doesn't come easily, requires incredible patience that does not come naturally to him, is tremendously technical in a way that's foreign to him, and requires endurance in that he has to stand in one spot for hours. It's just another approach to making himself focus ruthlessly and one that gives him a huge reward for doing so: "Feeling the tug on the line is like putting the jumper cables on God. It's a direct charge. You get one of those a week and you feel recharged."

Know That Focus Helps You Figure Out What's Next

Activity without progress is running in place. Tactics without strategy are random acts. Focus keeps you running somewhere; it keeps your efforts pointed in a particular direction.

In all of the sports he tried and tried hard to be good at, bobsledder Kirby Best has always gotten his greatest satisfaction out of anything that makes him go fast. He feels that functioning in a high-speed environment provides him with "ultimate focus, and requires particular efficiency in thinking and movement—and Kirby values efficiency: "When I go to do something, I do it. I don't waste a lot of time."

Despite his success on the Canadian bobsled team, Kirby really had his eyes on another prize. He thought there was another sport in which he could go even faster. "I always wanted to be a Formula One driver. It's what took me into bobsledding. [The Formula One folks] always took the rookie-of-the-year bobsled driver and gave him a test drive in a Formula One car. I thought my ticket to Formula One was bobsledding."

In 1979, Kirby Best was rookie of the year. Unfortunately, they weren't offering rides anymore.

The goal never disappeared, though. Kirby knew what was next; he knew what he had to do. As of today, he has taken nine high-speed driving courses.

Trust That Focus Takes You Out of Panic Mode

Pilot Bob Stangarone, vice president of corporate communications for Cessna Aircraft, doesn't acknowledge he has had emergencies. He says he's had two or three situations where he was "on the edge of an emergency." He is practiced at putting events into perspective on a daily basis—never having panic become the focal point of his thinking.

"I had a twin-engine failure at 7,000 feet over Long Island in a snowstorm. One engine stopped. A minute later the other engine stopped. It was zero-zero right to the ground. Before we declared an emergency, we figured out that it was snow blocking the air intakes on the engines. We were able to select an alternate air source and get the engines restarted. We weren't getting full power, because the engines weren't getting all the air they needed, but at least we had about 80 percent. We found a place called Kennedy International Airport and landed there. As we were going over the threshold, we could see a 747 sitting at a right angle to the runway, getting ready to take the runway. You could see the front of the aircraft, but not the back—that's how heavy the snow was."

The primary business lesson of events like this is one named by athlete-executives from surfers like Izzy and Coco Tihanyi to climbers like Stacie Blair and Mark Richey to pilots like Bob Stangarone and Mike Angiulo: don't panic. Bob put it in pilot parlance: "Fly the airplane and stay calm."

The last thing you want to do is get tense, because then you develop tunnel vision and you start to lose sight of your options. You want to work with your brain, not against it. A type of temporal distortion kicks in, which I speculate is one of our survival instincts. Time seems to slow down, allowing you to process options carefully in an extreme, high-intensity environment. If you have ever faced a life-and-death situation, it's likely you've described this phenomenon to other people. It takes you a lot longer in "real time" to tell the story of how you made the right choice and survived than it did for your brain to process the options. Bob experienced the same thing over Long Island in that snowstorm.

In the airplane you revert to your checklists and your training to keep moving and stave off panic. In a business situation it's very similar. You have certain tools, certain resources. You have a team behind you.

During his career in aviation, which has included senior corporate communications positions with aircraft manufacturers Rolls-Royce North America and Sikorsky Aircraft, Bob occasionally had a need to activate certain types of "crisis teams," primarily in the aftermath of accidents. One incident involved Hussein bin Talal, king of Jordan, a good customer of Sikorsky's, who was in the United States and decided to take his entourage to the Sikorsky plant.

The morning of the scheduled visit, a call came from the FAA: one of the helicopters had crashed.

King Hussein was himself a helicopter pilot, and he hadn't liked the weather conditions, so he took a motorcade down to Connecticut. The four Sikorsky employees on board the other helicopter died in a fiery crash in the mountains.

"It sounds like an aviation problem, but it's really a business thing. Not only did we have to handle the relationship with the king when he arrived, because he didn't know anything about it, but we also had to handle the news media, protocol demands—it was a very broad issue."

Bob says the transferable lesson from his experiences "on the edge of emergency" is that sequential nature of solving the problem, which can be done only with a cool head. In his situation over Long Island, he analyzed the problem and concluded that the engines failed because they weren't getting fuel, spark, or air. He went through the checks to determine which one was the likely cause. Fuel system indicators told him that fuel was going to the engine. His electrical system appeared to be working. Based on that, he concluded the problem was air, and that led to another set of checks related to the air. And all of this occurred in about a minute. Again, the phenomenon of temporal distortion seems to support an amazing level of brain and physical action if you don't panic.

With the King Hussein situation, Bob had the press outside clamoring for answers, uninformed customers arriving at the plant during a maelstrom, the need to brief the king, and the need to tell employees who have just lost coworkers and friends. A happy day turned really bad. And then for him personally, it was the loss of four people who were his good friends and colleagues.

He followed the same process as for restarting his failed engines: Collect the facts. Have a logical sequence to take action. Take action. In this case, for someone in Bob's position, the sequence is that you open your mouth only after you have collected the facts, sorted them through, and prepared a statement. You see people after a disaster like this making the sequence mistake all the time: they speak from emotion and not information. People want answers and direction in a crisis. They need to get information in such a way that suggests you do have a checklist to solve the problem and that you are, in fact, going through that roster of actions.

The situation Bob faced unfolded so rapidly that, without a crisis plan in place, coordinating the actions of people around him—ensuring that the whole team maintained focus—would have exacerbated the challenge:

"We had been preparing for the king's visit for several days, working internally with our protocol, media relations, and logistics people. There was considerable interface with the Secret Service, which is responsible for head-of-state visits.

"The day before the visit, we sent two S-76 helicopters to Massachusetts to fly the king and his entourage down to Stratford, Connecticut. The weather the next morning was pretty severe, so the group decided to come down by motorcade.

"About 8:00 A.M., I was in my office and received a call from the CEO telling me to immediately come to his office. Several company executives were on the speakerphone with the FAA. The message was that one of our helicopters, which decided to return that morning with two pilots and two maintenance personnel, had dropped off the radar. A few minutes later there were reports of a crash in the wooded mountains along the route of flight. At that point I assembled my communications team, which included our protocol, media relations, and logistics people, to let them know the situation and prepare for the worst. A little later we had reports confirming that the aircraft had in fact crashed, at which point we activated our crisis plan.

"Since the press was aware of the king's visit, we were already getting press calls that morning. We held back any comments about the visit and the accident until we could meet with the king to discuss and get his concurrence on how we would handle it. Our protocol and security people were the primary interface with the Secret Service. Our media relations team developed proposed talking points to use with the media at the appropriate time. When the motorcade arrived, we immediately went into a conference room to explain the situation to the king and proposed how we would handle it. We knew that assassination would be high on the list of press interest. (Over the years there had been several attempts on the king's life.)

"I don't recall when the media found out about the crash, but as soon as they did, we had dozens of reporters, including networks, at our front gate. Meanwhile, we worked out a statement for the press. I recall sending sandwiches out to the press while we conducted our meeting because it took a couple of hours to understand the situation and develop a response that was in everyone's interest.

"At about noon, I went out to the press gathering at the front gate and gave them the statement and answered some basic questions, being sure not to speculate on the cause of the accident. It was particularly difficult because those on the aircraft were people I'd worked with over several years. (We did not release the identities at that point because positive ID had not been made and next of kin was not yet notified.)

"Over the next few days the press speculated further on the possibility of an assassination attempt, and there was some 'evidence' to support that. We worked with the Secret Service over the next few weeks in their investigation, recounting every action leading up the accident. In the final analysis, an assassination attempt was ruled out.

"To this day, the NTSB has not officially determined a probable cause of the accident."

If you don't panic, you keep your emotions at bay. Your cognitive function—your focus—remains dominant. You can make sense. You can handle the crisis.

PART 2

TEAM LEADERSHIP

CHAPTER 13

Team Elite Is
Not Just a Name:

Your Team Is Critical

THE ELEMENTS OF personal excellence covered in Part 1 surfaced in two ways during the interviews. First, the athlete-executives revealed them in stories about their adventures; second, they cited them specifically as success lessons in their careers. This might lead you to wonder where certain other characteristics might show up—like intelligence, humor, empathy.

These traits are here and abundantly evident in the executives' interactions with their teams. They tend to talk about intelligent decisions as the product of collective intelligence, and they talk about enjoyable work environments as the invention of the people who work there.

This section on team leadership shows the success lessons in play in a way that affects the work environment and elicits the very best from the team. And when *team* refers to a group of focused, passionate individuals, rather than a collection of people who simply work for the same department or company, everyone can take credit for those success lessons.

The core message of this chapter comes out of the fact that in any fair competition a team of high performers will always outperform a group of high performers.

A team has a coordinated energy that gives it an inherent strength over people connected only by titles, divisions, or proximity. A group is a collection of people artificially brought together to function for a common purpose. They are résumés come to life, a bunch of possibly skilled workers whose efforts are orchestrated through a system of objectives and organizational charts. In contrast, a team is a collection of individuals who are inspired to work together. Maybe they were a collection of résumés when they were first hired, but something happened to give them a common sense of purpose that they find truly motivating.

You want to build a team of people who are extraordinary enough—through good leadership—to work together effectively while retaining their personalities and egos.

As Shellye Archambeau, CEO of MetricStream, states, "The number-one trait of an organization that is likely to succeed? Once you've done your due diligence, it's the team. Even if you start out with a business plan that has a little flaw, or a market that may not be right, if you have a strong team, you can maneuver yourself into success. You can change the overall value proposition."

Versus television head Gavin Harvey adds that you should forget the mentality of hiring a top performer to save the day. Everyone on the team needs to contribute and to expect that the individuals will collectively prove to be top performers.

I am a member of a skydiving group called Team Elite. We stop being a group of some of North America's best skydivers and start being a team sometime on the first day of our annual four-day gathering. Our aim at this event is to build extremely challenging formation skydives. After the first few jumps we start to reconnect in a way that makes Team Elite more than a name. When we leave one another, we go back to our home drop zones and do what we can to help jumpers on the way up hone their skills and join the ranks of top performers, but those of us who work hard to earn and keep our membership on Team Elite cannot do the same formations at our home drop zones that we do together—no matter how good we are. Not because each of us is so individually talented, but because the aggregate talent on the team is so substantial and we have been effectively inspired to excel both by our personal aspirations and our leaders. We transition from a group to a team.

Team Elite has a high staffing threshold; we do things together that we can do only with this specific team. Individual talent and desire make a group. Once inspired to excel jointly, we have a team.

Never Compromise on Hiring Decisions

First rule of hiring: Do not cut corners. If you do, you will pay for it again and again, and so will everyone else who works for you. "I think this person is okay; we'll give him a try" is not the way to approach it.

The truth is you have to compromise on many things to succeed in business. Perfection is rarely an option. Limited time and resources do not allow for it. But it is critical that hiring not be one of the areas where you compromise. Put 100 percent effort into hiring so that you are confident you have the right person.

One of the biggest costs of doing business is often the cost of employee turnover. Business & Legal Reports (www.BLR.com) has created a calculator to determine the cost of replacing an employee, which can be 30 percent of annual compensation or even higher. The topics in the matrix cover three major areas: cost factors for the department, which focuses on compensation; cost factors for HR, or whoever has the lead in the hiring process; and other costs in

Gavin Harvey, president and CEO of Versus TV, climbing in the French Alps on the Alpe D'Huez stage of the Tour de France course

www.PhotoBreton.com, 2006

total dollars such as placement agency fees, testing, and training. And then there's the cost of lost productivity, if you have a way of determining that.

Everyone you hire should have two critical traits: judgment and follow-through. These are absolutes. Do not compromise on these two mandatory traits.

The level and type of judgment you would expect from a receptionist is different from that of the senior executive, but judgment must nonetheless be present or you'll have work disruptions to deal with and maybe even security issues. One requisite aspect of judgment is the willingness, and hopefully also the ability, to work out conflict.

You will forever have to micromanage someone who lacks both judgment and follow-through. Without judgment, the person will either make poor decisions, which someone in the organization will have to fix, or constantly go to someone else to make decisions for him. And there is not enough time in the day to follow around someone who doesn't deliver. A person with follow-through has a sense of accountability for his commitments. He has something to prove: mainly that he'll do what he says he'll do. With that trait present, you have reason to believe that your example of taking personal responsibility for consequences of that follow-through will be emulated.

With those two factors evident, you can move to organization-specific traits. Assess the person far beyond the talents presented in the résumé. Presumably the person has skills that match the needs of the organization; otherwise you shouldn't be talking to her in the first place. Beyond that, she has to have a personality, disposition, and risk profile that fits in with the rest of the organization.

This cultural match is vital. One of my former colleagues recruited someone she had worked with in another environment to work for her at her new job. They had been a great team with complementary skill sets and compatible work styles. In a very short time after the hiring, it became evident to my colleague that she had made a mistake. The person she had recruited did not fit into the culture of her new organization and, as a consequence, felt isolated. My colleague did this person no favors for another reason: because that new hire was a mismatch, when another position with more responsibility and better salary opened up, her sterling credentials got her only a perfunctory interview. The position she was hired for was a dead-end career move. It was never a matter of whether she would leave the company; it was only a matter of when. Turnover was built into that hiring decision.

Among the compatibility elements you want to identify is a risk profile that's consistent with the rest of the organization, unless you've made a conscious decision that that isn't necessary for the particular position. By risk profile, I mean that every organization has a certain risk quotient. The problem with having employees with a risk quotient that is significantly out of line with the organization is that you may find yourself with someone who has all the right skills for your company but can't possibly be the kind of team player you aimed to find.

Figuring that out starts with determining the personality of your organization. Describe your organization in terms of personality traits using any one of a number of descriptions out there—or make up your own. Here's one cut:

- ◆ Strategic, strong-willed, and independent
- ◆ Empathetic—you hear "Kumbaya" in the corridors
- ◆ Reliable and steady, turning to proven methodologies first when there's a problem to solve
- ◆ Action-oriented and going for the gusto—change is an opportunity

Intensity, sense of humor, sociability, and risk inclination surface in different ways with people—and organizations—that might be characterized in these four sample categories. The more correlation there is between what the people are and what the organization is, the more comfortable the people will be in the organization. And I don't mean comfortable in a pejorative sense—that is, lazy because everything is so familiar. I mean comfortable in the sense that they can start the job at a run from day one. They can, and will, propose ideas right after they sign the W-9. The more they fit, the more they will be inspired to perform and contribute and the less likely they will be to depart.

Early in my skydiving career, I wanted to go to a training camp for people who intended to excel in the sport. I needed a minimum of 70 jumps to qualify. Since I had just started jumping a few months before, I set out a plan to reach that jump count and did it just in time. I was under the impression that how many skydives I did and how well I performed on a jump were the primary criteria for succeeding on a skydiving team. From the pros at the camp I learned something quite different. They told us it was more important to pick teammates on the basis of personality, disposition, and commitment than ability. You can't train the first three into someone, but there's a lot you can do to escalate ability.

I'm not suggesting that you hire people without the appropriate training and background for the role in which they'll be cast, but out of the pool of people with the right qualifications, find the ones who fit with your organization. The best metaphor we heard in interviews about this issue came from the mountaineers. On an expedition lasting anywhere from days to weeks to months, they are sleeping next to their teammates, as well as climbing with them, eating with them, and trusting them to watch one another's back. They stressed the need to do that with someone with a similar level of motivation and compatible disposition.

Other factors help too. One mountaineer-executive joked about a fellow member of an expedition having an unfortunate distinctive smell. At least there are quick ways to get rid of that incompatibility.

Never Forget That Your Team Is Only as Strong as Its Weakest Link

They also said these exact words: "Your team is only as strong as your weakest link," and that applies to any organization. Bill Baker, who holds a doctorate in industrial psychology in addition to his credits as a polar explorer and pioneer in public television, even went a little further with this. He tags the secret of success as having the right people: "One weak link is disastrous."

The presence of a weak link places a burden on everyone else to cover for him or invest an inordinate amount of resources in making up for his deficiency. That has a negative impact not only on the performance of the organization but also on morale.

Use the hiring process to get A players. Victims are never A players and don't belong on your team. An 80-mile-an-hour wind, freezing temperatures, a blinding blizzard, and you're stuck on a mountain with someone complaining about the weather. And then she says, "Wish I'd gone with the Brits. They had sunshine the whole way." Your life is potentially in the hands of someone who sees herself as a victim of bad weather, bad timing, and being born non-British. This scenario is unlikely, of course, since mountaineers vet each other carefully before heading upward for a few weeks with someone. But in offices all over the world, we have to deal with people like this as coworkers, clients, and customers.

Mountaineer Kevin Sheridan, founder and CEO of HR Solutions, says there are three classes of employees. Based on his research, this is where they fall:

+ **Engaged.** These people are mentally energized and committed to the mission, vision, and values of the organization. Twenty-five percent of the workforce falls into this category; employers would describe these employees as people who always go above and beyond. They care about the customer, the quality of their work, and the organization. They are can-do people.

+ **Ambivalent (not engaged).** They are "checked out." They lack spirit and vivacity; they feel unappreciated and insignificant. Kevin puts the percentage of the workforce who fit here at 59, which means that more than half the people going to work every day might be considered merely average. They are not can-do people, but they're not victims either.

+ **Disengaged.** These are the people you don't want to be around. They have negative energy; they focus on problems. Sixteen percent are these "watercooler malcontents." This is the actively disengaged population, which is full of victims. To them it's always someone else's fault. They are not willing to accept responsibility for their actions; they fight feedback tooth and nail. One of Kevin's clients calls them "terrorists" because of how they insidiously disrupt the organization.

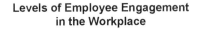

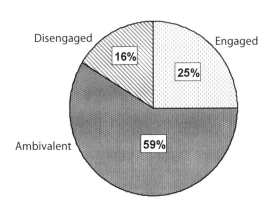

Source: HR Solutions' National Employee Study

© 2008 HR Solutions

What do you do with the employees in the disengaged category? Move them out of your organization. Better yet, make sure you never hire them in the first place.

Build a Magnetic Culture

Kevin is sharing his concept of a Magnetic Culture so you can reap some of the benefits of his years of success in advising companies on hiring. The term describes an environment that draws talented employees to the workplace and sustains an environment in which they are less likely to leave, so you reduce your employee turnover.

At the heart of the Magnetic Culture are engaged employees. Kevin's research shows you can characterize these desirable people as being the following:

- ◆ Loyal
- ◆ Motivated
- ◆ Committed

- Driven by their job content
- An inspiration to others; positive people
- Optimistic
- Supportive of coworkers
- Oriented to providing good customer service

In conversations with Kevin and other interviewees about creating teams consisting of these people with passion, discipline, and the other success traits—all of those covered in Part 1, on personal excellence—they offered tips on vetting candidates so you do not get stuck with C players:

- Involve multiple people in the process. Before the candidate gets to you, have a subject-matter expert evaluate the person's skills and experience, another person address administrative matters like salary and benefits, and someone else focus on character and personality. Then get them all together in the same room to offer their thoughts. This is way too important to handle by e-mail. Remember: 80 percent of communication is nonverbal. E-mail is a powerful tool, but it is not suited to vital conversations on critical issues.
- When the candidate arrives at what may be the last interview, it is time for questions like these: "What do you consider your greatest accomplishment?" "What are your career goals?" "What's your concept for an ideal team?"
- When the candidate gets to you, use the conversation to steer toward a few questions that will either affirm choosing this person or send up red flags. It doesn't matter if you ask some of the same questions as the other interviewers. If you get one answer and they get another, that in itself is a problem. Examples of baiting questions:
    - *Who did you meet with before you made it to me?* You want a clear answer like "John in engineering, Keisha in HR, and Greg in marketing." An answer like "John in engineering, somebody in HR, I think her name was Kasha, and a tall, bald man" is a red flag.
    - *Why did you leave your first job after only six months?* The point of this question is to ascertain how the person handles implied criticism. An answer like "My boss drove me nuts, and they stuck me

in a cubicle next to the lunchroom, which smelled like burritos" is a red flag. This person has a victim mentality.

◆ *What are your three biggest success factors?* You want to know whether you are compatible with this person and whether this person is on the same wavelength with the rest of your team. Your biggest three being passion, discipline, and persistence, and the candidate's being a manageable workload, feeling comfortable with assigned tasks, and pleasant coworkers is a red flag. You're climbing K2, and he's going for a walk in the park.

World-class race car driver Don Bell, founder and CEO of Bell Micro-products, points out that, even with a good vetting process, some people will come out looking average compared to the powerhouses. A team including these "average" people can be a superior unit, though, as long as it has no weak links. There is a difference between A players and superstars. Not everyone on the team needs to be a superstar. In many cases, having a mother lode of superstars would work against you. But in the positions where you need one, don't compromise.

At the core of this lesson is the belief that people can rise significantly above what they think they are capable of if they simply set their expectations higher. Bell scored many successes in his long career, but he credits others, particularly teams, as the reason. A prime example comes from his early days at a company where "We had massive success as a team of people." Don ran into one of the sales managers at that company about 10 years later.

"What made us so successful?" he wondered.

Don told him, "We had a good team, Joe."

"No, Don, we were average," he retorted.

"Yeah, but you didn't know it, did you?"

"Average" guys comprised an extraordinary team. They believed they could win. Whatever happened, they would be the victor. The truth is, the only thing "average" about them was that they were average among high performers. It's like saying that someone who barely made it into Mensa has an average intellect.

Summarizing the route to building a Magnetic Culture, Kevin Sheridan offers these 10 tips, all of which are explored further in this and other chapters relating to team leadership and excellence:

- ◆ Provide career development opportunities.
- ◆ Pay competitive salaries.
- ◆ Allow flexible work schedules.
- ◆ Provide desired job content.
- ◆ Provide top-notch customer service.
- ◆ Ensure that the company mission is clear.
- ◆ Retain the best supervisors and managers.
- ◆ Supply strong senior management.
- ◆ Maintain a positive organizational culture.
- ◆ Offer generous benefits.

Give Your Team Members Permission to Push Back and Offer Their True Opinions

Encouraging employees to voice differing opinions will work smoothly with some people but seems to be misinterpreted by others as an invitation to get emotional.

In a heated conversation, particularly one about something that went wrong, people tend to step on each other's sentences. The outcome varies. The loud guy may prevail. Or maybe the person with the most authority sorts through the fragments of facts on the table and draws a conclusion. Building skydiving formations in free fall is quite difficult. The attempts are commonly not successful, and what went wrong may be a single thing or a series of things so minute that the free-fall videographer's camera didn't catch it; only the person who caused the problem or was next to the person who caused the problem might actually know something useful. A winning four-person team may shift from one formation to another 20 times in the 35-second time window given in competition skydiving, so there's a lot going on and myriad possibilities for error. David Becker, president and cofounder of PhilippeBecker, a San Francisco branding and packaging agency, learned a technique for communicating problems without confrontation while competing as part of Focus4, a top-ranked skydiving team. It was a technique that tracks to work that Dr. Bob Moore, an organizational and sports psychologist, introduced to the competitive skydiving community a few years before. Moore told them to pass the rock. People sit around a table or a circle or whatever they want. Whoever has the rock may speak freely—and everyone else must listen. (Some teams have adopted Bob's technique by adding the twist of allowing the person with the rock to speak only about his own performance.) Take this concept to the meeting room when things are tanking and pass the paperweight until everyone gets used to the idea of listening to other people until they are finished speaking.

Always Let Your Team Members Shine When They Succeed

A few years ago an organization that had hired me was going through a transition from the interim president to the new, permanent head of the association. The interim president had done a masterful job of reinforcing the group's financial position, and part of her success involved carefully selecting some new team members in the area of member services and program development.

A few members of the association knew what had transpired, but certainly not most of them. So when the new president took the stage to welcome several hundred members to the group's annual conference, and he only fleetingly acknowledged his predecessor, the widespread assumption was that she hadn't done all that much—except in the minds of those who knew the real story. Their private praise of her work grew in volume over the next two days, making the new president look like a bit of a fool by the end of the conference.

By failing to give credit to someone who had earned it, as well as to the great team she had put together, he inadvertently implied that all the progress and accomplishments of recent days and weeks should be credited to him. He missed an opportunity not only to raise the spirits of his staff but also to define the kind of personal brand that would have served him well in the long term.

Don't Be Afraid to Hire People Who Are Better than You

In contrast to that new president, Gavin Harvey puts the emphasis where it needs to be: "I'm focused on the goal. I'd rather lose credit for something as long as we hit the goal. If that happens, that's your credit. I don't need to be the person who came up with the brilliant idea and who has the best presentation—the focus should be on you if you did it. I'm not an egotist about that." This is like the driver who says "Thanks" when people congratulate him after a race and then adds, "but it was the pit crew that pulled it off."

Gavin even takes it a step further in indicating his preference for being in the company of winners. He's "okay being the guy who comes in last, because that means I'm competing with studs."

Say "Good-Bye" If You Must

Unproductive or disruptive behavior can take different forms, from the marginal performance of a slacker to the contrarian's constant, annoying "but what about . . . ?" One of the most insidious, however, comes from the person who nods and votes yes at a meeting while concurrently IMing a colleague outside the meeting with "OMG stupid move LOL."

What's necessary when you detect that behavior is a "coaching moment," according to former dressage competitor Shellye Archambeau, an Internet World Top 25 "Click and Mortar" executive. As the CEO of MetricStream, a company that helps companies avert regulatory nightmares, she has seen many situations where employee behavior like that can help move a company away from compliance with critical quality, government, or internal policies. You take the person aside, raise awareness of the problem, and describe the change in behavior that would improve the situation.

Hopefully coaching will reveal that the person is a talented individual who just doesn't have good interpersonal skills. Shellye cannot imagine speaking her mind except to her IM buddies. That means that coaching cannot take the form of a judgment and prescription for future behavior. It must involve an investigation of why this person, who at one point seemed like a good hire, sinks into communication mud whenever discussions involve disagreement or confrontation.

Maybe this person would contribute more to the company by not partici-pating in the decision-making meetings. Maybe any aspect of her job that involves a battle of ideas is where she shows her weakest side as a contribu-tor. Options: Shift her responsibilities so she doesn't feel the necessity to play double agent. Get her away from the meetings. Let her exercise her skills without forced "team" interaction.

That doesn't always work, of course, so after coaching comes the warning. After warning comes the separation. The destructive effect of a coworker operating with a kind of double-agent mentality cannot be exaggerated.

Hire as if your life depends on it. Choose to undertake your business venture only with people who deserve your trust, are competent, and have the ability to focus consistently on the right moves along the way to the goal, as well as on the goal. And view every person you hire as someone you are going to need to come through for you when all hell breaks loose.

CHAPTER 14

Why Doom Yourself to Failure?

Abhor Mediocrity and Average Behavior

"Always deliver your personal best. Lower standards will doom you to failure."

—Gord Woolley, Canadian Olympic Bobsled Team member and founder and president of Jessam Communications

"The only unknown is inside yourself. Ask yourself, 'Am I good enough today to get to the top?'"

—Chris Warner, mountaineer who has summited more than 150 times on peaks above 19,000 feet and founder/CEO of Earth Treks, Inc.

WHAT GORD LEARNED from his bobsledding days is:

Jason Schoonover, a fellow of the Explorers Club and leader of expedition canoe trips around the world, high on Saskatchewan's Churchill River

Malcolm Lawson, 2008

- He can apply his competitive nature every day to the benefit of himself and the people around him.
- The thrill of either winning or coming darned close is the same as the thrill of getting a large order. And it's not just the thrill of the order, but the fact that you have taken it from someone else: the client chose you over someone else. It's a clear win that can be measured.
- Make sure that team members shine. People want to know that they can be above average, so it's important to let them know when and how they have exceeded expectations.
- Knowing that you're winning does you good. Just having it in your head that you are so much better than the competition gives you huge advantages.

Gord's footnote to these success factors: "When I don't get an order, I'm pissed off."

There are plenty of people who are satisfied, or even happy, with being average. None of them is part of this book. There comes a point when you have to figure out if you are so comfortable with being average—that's who you are and that's all you believe you can do—that you do not have to force yourself beyond that level. But if "average" sounds like "mediocrity" to you, then keep moving through the lessons here.

Strive to Be the Best—and That Doesn't Mean the Best Among the Average

"It's okay if we're as good as everybody else" is not an acceptable strategy for success. If all you want to be is as good as everyone else in the industry, then that's all you will ever be. Gavin Harvey, head of Versus television, calls on the wisdom of his "gang" to sum it up: "In motorcycling, we have a saying, 'If you're not accelerating, you're decelerating.'"

I worked with a company recently that made it a corporate philosophy that whatever the rest of the industry was doing, they weren't going to do it quite like that. There had to be a better way, and they would find it. Not surprisingly, this company is both quite innovative and exceedingly successful.

Even companies that have to rely on a low-cost-provider strategy seek to differentiate themselves through production and distribution efficiencies that allow them to underprice the competition. It's difficult to use this model to achieve success in the long term, though. If all you are doing is producing a commodity that has nothing distinctive about it, and you spend all of your time figuring out how to make the same product or service less expensively, ultimately the person who wins is the one who figures out how to cut the most corners. Trying to be successful when your only competitive advantage is the lowest price is a very tough path. Unfortunately, this is the perennial challenge of any company that provides a product or service that is seen as a commodity available in identical form from many sources.

Much of the steel industry has been based on this strategy since its inception.

An automaker will go to multiple sources for the rolled steel that goes into its cars, and all it wants to know is who will sell the material that meets its specifications the least expensively. The steel producer does nothing more than do what it takes to underbid the competition. All that does is result in low margins, which leads to battles for market share, which lead to consolidation and then potentially to few enough producers that prices stabilize.

I followed a company that had adopted a low-cost-provider strategy to its sad and logical conclusion where it would lose business over a fraction of a percent of price. Its margins were horrible—less than 2 percent. In a down economy with multiple sources of both domestic and foreign competition, this is not where you want to be. You are like the man who is already skin and bones and now has to fight for food against hungry dogs.

The company had no proprietary knowledge, no unique intellectual capital.

You want to be able to do things better than anybody else, and that means you cannot be average. You cannot be mediocre.

You want to avoid falling into the commodities bucket and trying to succeed solely on price. Securities traders and life insurance salespeople found themselves dumped there in a relatively short period of time. What is the compelling reason to do a trade with a major brokerage house at thirty-five dollars when you can do it through a discount broker for seven dollars or less?

The major brokerage houses have all transitioned to an added-value model. The quality stockbrokers may even tell you that you really do not need them if all you want to do is initiate a trade. But if you want the benefit of their expertise, experience, and research departments, the additional cost of trading with them may be well worth it. Often they are certified financial planners or carry other significant certifications that make them readily capable of adding value.

Similarly, you can now buy life insurance on the Internet and never talk with anyone. To reclaim their competitive advantage, insurance companies had to begin requiring their agents to boost their financial planning credentials to provide a very real value-add in that industry.

In the speaking business, it's not uncommon for people to hope to become a professional speaker without having any distinguishing expertise or knowledge. They tell me of their interest in being a speaker, and I ask them, "What are you going to talk about?" And they say, "I don't know. What do people want to hear?"

So I revise the question: "What topic are you uniquely qualified to address?" People who cannot answer that question are going to have a difficult time succeeding. Without unique expertise, they have no competitive advantage. They are providing a commodity, and their fee structure will reflect it.

Print and online media covering the technology arena quickly found they were having a hard time differentiating themselves from other media sources. The rapid rate of change and development in the industry meant that a handful of "computer magazines" couldn't keep up. There are now hundreds of print magazines in the United States alone that are devoted to aspects of the industry so specific that dozens of them list circulation from between 150 and 900. I suppose there just aren't that many people beyond that number who would understand what they're talking about. They are well differentiated in the market, but that may not be a great model for making money.

That's usually true of an activity in which there are low barriers to entry. So now this trick of avoiding mediocrity through superior performance, intellectual capital, and market differentiation gets really complex. How do you do what the people in this book did, which is to combine those elements with a business model that yields strong revenues and good margins?

The short answer is that, for the most part, their businesses had a higher barrier to entry—businesses requiring access to capital and high-quality human resources and, as a corollary, to the intellectual property they offer. These athlete-executives knew that if they did what it took to succeed the rewards would likely be substantial.

The mentality of an extreme athlete is likely to go in this direction. They— and, actually, "they" include Maryann and me, who are both competitive extreme athletes as well as business professionals—are the uphill hikers. The people who relish the challenge so much that they find the struggle toward the goal to be part of the pleasure of achieving it.

In the case of Deidre Paknad, she's the uphill cyclist with an appetite for the tough ride. In her business of being the leading provider of legal holds and retention management solutions, she notes that "You have the choice every day to do something less than excellence, but you make a conscious choice toward excellence in your hiring, in your customers, and in every part of your business. We don't want customers just to be reasonably happy with what we produce; we want them to be crazy in love with it."

Believe in Yourself but Be Reasonable; You're Not a Superhero

Mountaineer Chris Warner has gripping stories in his climbing logs of people who tried to effect rescues of teammates and loved ones on Mt. Everest. In his book, *High Altitude Leadership*, he labels this flaw "lone heroism." He vividly makes the point that lone heroes jeopardize the lives of others on an expedition and, similarly, endanger organizations. By assuming too much responsibility for making a difference in a tough situation, they set themselves up as superheroes. Everyone else who needs to have a role in creating a solution, everyone else who has something valuable to contribute, is left behind as he flies off with his Superman cape flapping in the breeze.

That's not confidence; it's misguided effort, and if it happens repeatedly, it might also signal arrogance. Not a single athlete-executive we talked with listed arrogance as a success factor.

Deliver Your Personal Best

For marathoner Quang Pham, founder of Lathian Health, "You have to have pride in carrying your own weight." If that sounds a lot like a Marine Corps philosophy of delivering personal best, it's because it is. Quang's service in war and peacetime as a Marine lieutenant reinforced his innate desire to step up and be proud of the fact that he could reach high standards of performance. When he had not quite hit the number of hours that the Corps said he should have to fly a medivac helicopter in a war zone, but the opportunity to do so arose, he realized hours were not the issue. The bigger question that the Corps really wanted the answer to was "Do you have the ability to deliver the troops where they need to be?" He assured them he did, which prompted the orders he wanted: "Then the job's yours."

Quang's pride in his ability to do the job was rooted in self-awareness, which is the link between desire to do your best and knowing what your best actually is. Lathian Health reflects the same clear perception of capability and high standards for outcome. Quang's pioneering efforts in bridging the pharmaceutical industry with the community of health-care providers online, rather than via a rep showing up at the door, inherently involved lots of problems. From the pharmaceutical companies' perspective, he had to overcome doubts about effectiveness; from the health-care providers' view, he had to get past concerns about misrepresentation. He managed to exceed expectations, assuring both sets of parties that they were in good virtual hands.

Prepare for the Outcome You Are Seeking

Aerobatic pilot and paragliding pioneer Mike Angiulo learned the intricacies of proper preparation the hard way—fortunately, reining in some of his brasher instincts before he either killed himself or took them to Microsoft, where they might have made his career short-lived.

In 1998, Mike had a new hot-rod paraglider that he'd been flying in relatively mild air in Washington state. A paraglider is a large fabric wing, a bit like a giant parachute, with a harness beneath it that holds the pilot. Mike decided to try paragliding with his new gear in Mexico, where the air had more rock and roll to it than up north. He got into extreme turbulence, overcontrolled the paraglider, got it tangled, and found himself in free fall far from any hospital or helipad. He threw out a little reserve parachute just before he came crashing down on a group of hundred-foot ponderosa pines. The last thought that went through his head when he faced his death was that he would never see his girlfriend again. It was a sad realization that made his plight real. Not a religious moment. Not a fear of pain. But the thought that he had seen his girlfriend for the last time. As he crashed through the trees, huge limbs snapped off. Finally, his glider got hung up in pieces of the tree and slowed his fall enough so that, when he crashed into a steep hill and tumbled down, he had nothing worse than a twisted ankle. At that moment he decided to ask his girlfriend to marry him. He got on a plane for home the next day, and that's exactly what he did. It was not the outcome he'd specifically prepared for, but he's been delighted with it ever since.

Mike didn't immediately learn the difference between a risk and a risk well taken, though. He also broke his leg trying to win in a spot-landing contest. The target was a cone in the middle of the desert. Instead of landing softly five feet away from it, he stretched out his glide and reached out his leg and snapped it in half. He won the contest and finally learned his lesson, moving to certified aircraft after that.

He discovered that, with the proper training and all the right decision making, flying inverted, flying at lower than 100 feet, and hitting negative Gs does not have to be excessively dangerous. In fact, flying planes like a Pit Special, one of which he owned for a few years, does not have a higher fatal-accident rate than a general aviation trainer. "The difference is that all of the variables have to be exactly right, and you have to have a higher level of currency. As long as I could control those variables, I was excited to do the world-class stunts." Having had some taste of the downside of not being prepared for the risk, as soon as he lost the currency and the edge, he knew it was time to quit.

After becoming regional champion in the Northwest region in the sportsman category in 2003, Mike said good-bye to the Pit and put his acumen for risk taking into projects at Microsoft. One of the carryover benefits for Microsoft is Mike's keen ability to set priorities for his division.

Be Persistent but Patient

"Good decisions over time" is how marathoner Dennis Sponer of ScripNet sees the parallels between the level of persistence and consistency he has to have in both running and business. The patience is in waiting for the decisions to pay off, because he knows they will.

"I know when I plan to run in a marathon how many miles I have to log a week to be ready. Same thing in business. It's being prepared for later."

Patience plays a particularly significant role when nothing feels right. "Sometimes you go out for a run and your body doesn't cooperate, but you keep at it, and eventually your body comes along. In business you have similar breaks." Visions of going to sales meetings you don't want to be at pop into his head. The most vivid instances occurred when he started Scrip-Net. As much as he needed contracts with a number of pharmacies so they would accept the company's pharmacy card, the meetings seemed more like a chore than an opportunity because of all those who were not interested in working with a start-up. After repeatedly making the *Inc.* 500 due to its consistent rate of net sales growth, Dennis's persistence—and patience—seem well worth it.

Microsoft VP Kirill Tatarinov has a somewhat different challenge that requires the same formula. In his job as a corporate vice president, he spends all his time with people, and that daily experience has convinced him that patience is one of the key traits he needs to be successful. "When I started the corporate journey, I was a lot less patient than I am today," he admits, and so he had to train himself because, he believes, patience is something you learn. So the benefit he gets from teaching skiing through the Outdoors for All program is not just the enjoyment of seeing kids with learning disabilities raise their competence level on the slopes; it's also the patience he needs for work. He learns as the kids learn.

Accept that major outcomes may not occur quickly. Patience and persistence need to be joined together because one without the other will not get you where you want to go. Persistence without patience will drive everyone around you nuts, and patience without persistence will yield sporadic and possibly random outcomes.

There is an interesting balance point between people who are ambitious and people who understand that things can't necessarily happen overnight. How that plays out depends a lot on the organization you're part of. You have to be respectful of the people around you. If you belong to an organization known for moving gradually, you either have to know when to dial it back or leave. Pushing hard and fast all the time could well isolate you. That doesn't mean you cannot serve the organization at all. You could be a change agent, but you have to do it in a thoughtful way to avoid being too out of sync with everyone around you. "Change agent" is a precarious role. Unless you have substantial, inviolate authority, the knives will come at you sooner or later. When you force people out of their comfort zone, you are a threat. People will not forget what you did.

I worked with one midsized company with significant psychographic uniformity. It became clear to me very quickly that the people who worked there had a similar mind-set in terms of their sense of urgency and acceptance of change. This homogeneity has become as much a keystone of their success program as hiring people with the right skill set.

With the company executives' full support, I did an anonymous online survey to determine how the employees of this company respond to constant, ongoing change. On a scale of 1 to 10, with 1 being "I find constant change threatening and dispiriting" and 10 being "I thrive on constant change," the average for this group was 6.7. This is extremely high. I have asked a lot of audiences this question, and the majority of people rank their comfort level with change much lower. So what this survey documented is that the company has found a unique group of people who embrace change more than the norm.

Rapid success is a wonderful thing, and there is certainly nothing wrong with a high growth rate. But the fact is, things usually happen more gradually than overnight. And, from industry to industry, "overnight" has different meanings. I was watching a college football game recently, and one of the coaches, who had been at the school for five years, now has a solid program. One of the commentators said that he'd been there long enough to be an overnight success. Countless actors have spent decades working diligently and wallowing in anonymity until they become an "overnight success."

In the hundreds of organizations I've worked with, there is always an old guard and a new guard, and the difference often manifests in the contrasting pace at which they go for a goal. Sometimes the old guard is composed of people who have been there for more than six months, and sometimes it's many years. Regardless of duration, these people talk about "how we used to do it." People do all kinds of things to create a comfort zone, and that's one of the things they do. The breadth of the dividing line between the old guard and the new guard is a function of how rapidly the organization is changing. In a healthy organization, they can learn the lessons of persistence and patience from each other.

Persevere, with a Plan

Jason Schoonover is a fellow of the Explorers Club, that is, someone recognized by this prestigious professional society as having made documented contributions to exploration or scientific knowledge. He is also a leader of expedition canoe trips around the world. But with all of this high adventure in his life, he prepared himself to take business risks by exercising extraordinary caution. Earning good money through his management position at the second-largest radio station in Canada as well as a DJ business and freelance writing, he saved obsessively so that he could invest. He kept track of daily expenditures and has them in a frame in his fishing room. One weekend in 1975 he went to the movies and spent 25 cents on a bus, 25 cents on popcorn (the movie was free), and 17 cents for shoelaces. He did that for "three years, three months, and three weeks." And then he started investing in real estate.

Jason had three reasons for choosing real estate: "You do not make money being an employee and making money for somebody else. I also found out that more millionaires are made in real estate than any other endeavor on the planet. And then, I also wanted independence." Regarding the latter, he did not want something that would tie him to an office or store and to employees. His plan, which he promptly carried out through Schoonover Properties, was to buy real estate that would generate revenue and then put it under professional management.

"I've always planned the total arc of my life," says Jason, whose long-term plan has played out exactly as he'd hoped. Since falling in love with canoeing at the age of 10, Jason has paddled rivers from above Sweden's Arctic Circle to Southeast Asia and the Amazon in furious white water and led canoe expeditions on old fur trade and exploration routes in his native Canada. As a field collector of cultural artifacts, he has contributed pieces to museums around the world as well as to private collections.

Don't Kill Yourself Trying: Make Time to Relax and Savor

When your work truly engages your passion, it's tempting to do it all the time. We tend to applaud people in our society who achieve enormous success as they live and breathe their careers. The practical reason for introducing nonwork elements into your life is to make sure you don't hamper your effectiveness. If you become truly unidimensional, it can become very hard to relate to and interact with other people. What questions will you ask them to put yourself on the path to a nonwork conversation, which is something you always want to be able to have, even with colleagues and customers? The normal response to encountering someone who is totally absorbed in one topic or activity is to tune him out, unless you happen to have the same fascination for the topic or activity.

Despite the enormous daily pressures on him—as well as his reputation for both delivering and exacting high standards at Microsoft—Kirill Tatarinov skis every weekend during the season. His devotion to teaching kids with disabilities to ski through the Outdoors for All program adds a dimension to his time on the slope that goes beyond recreation, though. He sees distinct work-related benefits both to skiing purely for fun and in teaching challenged athletes. It's not only part of their overall maturing and development; it's also part of his own. The experience gives him a chance to cultivate patience, which he asserts is integral to influencing people.

His insight: "You limit yourself and the breadth of your success as an entrepreneur unless you can exercise patience and reach people effectively."

Consider all the variations and requirements of stomping mediocrity into the ground and heading up the hill. You want to strive to be the best, but not kill yourself—or anyone else—with your heroism. You want to understand how to deliver your personal best, but be scrupulous about what you drive toward. You want to be persistent, but that's no good without patience and a plan. Finally, if you really want to rise above average, you must take the opportunity to savor life.

CHAPTER 15

Wear Gloves If Your Hands Are Cold:

Eliminate the Victim Mentality

VICTIMS LET EVENTS dictate outcomes. Nothing bad is ever their fault.

As a child, you probably heard the biblical wisdom "The truth shall set you free." And then you found that's not always true. You ended up in the kiddie version of the supermax when you admitted to slamming a home run through your parents' bedroom window. Instead of spending your evening with a video game and banana split, you faced a corner in the living room—dessertless. If only you had laid the blame on that boy visiting the neighbors who live two blocks away. No one would have gotten hurt, and you'd have had your ice cream. Pointing your finger at the other guy would have been the smooth way to keep your life on track.

Let's not make well-intentioned parents solely responsible for watering that psychological weed called the victim mentality. Plenty of people, a lot of them on the cover of magazines, taught you by example that you could get away with stuff by diminishing your accountability.

Choose Your Associates Carefully; Victims Are Losers

Victims are losers, and their presence in business disrupts the productivity of people around them. Victims reduce productivity and can demoralize their colleagues.

We've all seen how victims behave and at some point maybe even made excuses for their lame behavior. A broken home, serious illness, loss of a loved one, alcoholic or drug-addicted parent, a poverty-stricken childhood—each and every one a good reason for pity. But we all know people who had one, or even all, of those trials in life who quashed the victim mentality. They provide insights and tools for the rest of us to do the same whenever "Why me?" creeps into our consciousness.

As a boy going through the process of his family's disintegration, Kevin Sheridan was kidnapped by his father. His mother had left him and his siblings home alone for a month; the oldest of the four was 12 at the time. The dad turned to his second wife and said, "I can't knowingly let my children grow up this way." An Illinois police officer suggested he kidnap the children because he had gone through a similar situation and, in playing by the letter of the law, lost his kids in court. Kevin's dad flew to their town and made some fatherly excuse to pick them up at school. Kevin's father had resettled on a Native American reservation in northern Wisconsin, and so that's where he took them. In conjoining his first family with his second, as well as the children of his wife's first marriage, Kevin's father brought the family total to nine kids overnight. Dad had grown up on the south side of Chicago in a very integrated neighborhood, so from his vantage point the situation on the reservation wasn't disturbing. Even though many of the families on the reservation who were white sent their kids to the "white" school 20 miles away, his dad would have nothing of that. Kevin and his siblings attended the tribal school, which he describes as "a helluva shock."

For two and a half years, other kids at school beat him up every day because he was not part of a tribe. He remembers that they kicked, spit on, hit, and pinched him; with tongue in cheek he describes it as "a character-building experience." But he means it. It was a time for him to figure out not only how to survive but also how to thrive. It was a delicate time for him, forcing him to do strange things like deliberately flunk seventh-grade math so he wouldn't have to go out for recess. Recess meant a guaranteed whooping.

But he abhorred victimhood, and that revulsion of the lie-down-and-die attitude churned a desire to rise up—not in anger but in achievement. Kevin eventually earned an M.B.A. from Harvard, started businesses, and is now CEO of HR Solutions International, based in Chicago. In his human relations consulting, his emphasis on both understanding and building diversity in the workforce carries unique weight. He knows firsthand what it is like to be a minority, and all the pain that can go with that, and feels it has made him a better management consultant. He also has lived the principle that overcoming discrimination can be done quite effectively without exploiting victimhood.

Quang Pham, marathoner, entre-

Kevin Sheridan, chief executive officer and chief consultant of HR Solutions, Inc., as he approaches the summit of Mt. Elbrus

Vern Tejas

preneur, and author of *A Sense of Duty: My Father, My American Journey*, faced the squinty eyes of judgment and skepticism when he pursued officer status in the U.S. Marine Corps. He wanted to thank the country that had helped him emigrate from South Vietnam at the age of 10 and present him and his family with opportunities he would not have had in his native land. Instead, some of the people he encountered in the Corps harbored the sense that Quang, whose father had served in the war as a pilot, was just the son of someone who "couldn't hold up his end of the war." Quang says that "Most people were rooting for me, but for some of them I was still the enemy. Look at how South Vietnamese were portrayed in a lot of the popular movies: inept, unwilling to fight, and on the wrong side."

Instead of acting like a victim, he served America like a hero. In 1990, when Desert Shield kicked off, the rules stated that there had to be two qualified night-vision-goggle pilots in the Marine helicopter to fly troops at night. When the war started, he was a first lieutenant with 320 hours in the cockpit and about 5 hours of night-vision-goggle experience—below the required experience threshold to fly the required missions. But when the wife of one of the fully qualified pilots became ill and the pilot was excused from duty, Quang volunteered, and the USMC put him to good use immediately. Quang's helicopter was one of the first Marine medivac helicopters to reach Kuwait City. He didn't have the hours, but he had the self-awareness of his skill to do the job.

Take Control of Your Destiny

Victimhood is a decision to allow circumstances and people to be an excuse for lesser performance than they are capable of. It all starts with the mind-set.

In a large skydiving formation, energy moves through the formation. Everyone in a formation of 100, 200, or 400 skydivers is experienced enough to know that you need to join the formation—called "docking"—without introducing any momentum into it. Doing otherwise would potentially destroy the formation. Unfortunately, with a skydive of that many people, that will almost never occur. While coming into the formation with too much speed should not happen, it's going to happen, so you just have to be prepared for someone making that mistake. You have to anticipate that waves of energy and movement will come through the formation as a result. If you don't contribute to dampening the waves, then you are not doing your job, and it's possible the formation will fall apart. If everyone takes responsibility for working to dampen the waves, the damage can be minimized or even averted.

You have a choice: contribute to solving the problem, even though you didn't cause it, or do nothing knowing that the formation will probably blow apart. It seems like an easy decision. But it is amazing how some people confronted with a problem they did not create will stand back instead of contributing to a solution. That is the victim mentality.

Lots of things "should not" happen in business, either, when you supposedly have the best team, good market conditions, a great plan, and everything else that sets you up for success. But shock waves will hit. Just know that. The mind-set of success becomes vitally important at that moment because it will trigger corrective actions. John Wilson, mountaineer and president and CEO of J.C. Wilson Associates, calls this contingency thinking. Contingency thinking reflects a comprehension of the things that can go wrong and knowing immediately what the corrective actions are for them. This does not imply obsessing over potential negatives but rather anticipating how you can respond to them (see Chapter 22).

Moving out of the victim mentality involves being proactive, not reactive. If you only respond to events, you will let events control you. If you take the initiative to stay ahead of events, you will be much more likely to craft the outcome you want to achieve.

A formation skydive with 35 people could potentially involve as many excuses as there are people for why it didn't work: There was traffic. Someone cut in front of me. There was someone below me I had to avoid. The aircraft were too far apart. The base was in a different place from the last four jumps.

There's a very simple solution to all these problems. The organizer gets everyone together and says, "And it will happen again, so if you want to be a world-class skydiver, handle it." The clear implication is that if you aspire to be a mediocre skydiver, then go ahead and let those things trip you up—and complain about them over a beer that night. However, if your aim is to make the *Guinness Book of World Records*, then do some contingency thinking and act accordingly.

Know That Successful Professionals Adapt

In a work environment, when the problem is a person, you have two choices: fix the relationship (i.e., adapt) or leave. The status quo is not acceptable; it isn't working. In fixing it, you may have to change the way you communicate, resolve differences, or do myriad other things to reduce friction and raise productivity. If you don't want to change, you should empty your desk and head to a different setting. What you know for sure is that the situation isn't working and that staying in it will do nothing positive for the company and nothing positive for you.

Eliminate the Excuses

Making excuses right before a competition is one way athletes mentally prepare for failure. One version is broadcasting ailments: "My hamstrings are sore." "The elevation has given me a wicked headache." In skydiving, jumpers often blame Mother Nature: "The sun was in my eyes."

In a formation skydive such as the one pictured here, people face different directions to create patterns in the air. Sometimes that means that early or late in the day a few of them will have the sun in their eyes. I can't count the number of times I've heard the sun blamed for a bad move that ruined the jump, so I now have a strategy for taking that excuse away. Before the jump,

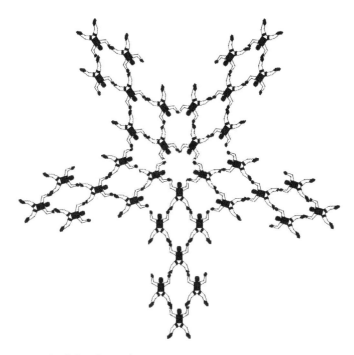

A 35-person skydiving formation

I simply tell some of the jumpers that the sun will be in their eyes. They should anticipate it, and we're never going to mention it again.

Grieve and Then Move On

After a string of injuries and comebacks, waterskiing champion Camille Duvall-Hero started working with a strength and conditioning coach, whom she credits with extending her career in the sport by years. She was skiing better than she ever had before and staying injury free. Then, at the age of 33, she had to leave the sport abruptly. She had a stroke. Camille says the quick disconnection from her sport because of "this ghost thing—something you couldn't see" meant that she "didn't get to say good-bye" to the sport in the manner she'd hoped.

Five-time world professional slalom champion. One of *Sports Illustrated*'s "100 Greatest Female Athletes of the Century." Winner of 15 U.S. waterskiing national titles. And then suddenly no more.

Camille learned that it's okay to be disappointed, but you "gotta feel that, let it rip, and get over it" and get back to work. After acknowledging that the central activity in her life was suddenly gone—that the stroke was a life-changing situation and she could not pretend that it hadn't happened—she knew she just had to figure out what to do with herself, with her other talents.

At first she found herself going on autopilot; she would go to the lake as if she were going to ski: "There was a grieving process. You have to go through that." After three months she withdrew from the lake for good. She was through it and moved on to a television career and then to the heights she now enjoys in the real estate business as a top broker in Manhattan.

Own Your Mind-Set

Once you've gotten rid of the excuses for failing, conquer two other mind-set issues: revisiting mistakes while the event is going on and anticipating trouble.

Athletes in all sports understand the directive from tennis coaches: "Don't play the last shot." During meetings, watch how people try to undo a bad move; all they do is make it worse. They crack a joke that isn't funny, so they crack another one, thinking maybe the laughs will finally come. They stumble over a concept being discussed, so they drag the conversation into territory that is more intellectually familiar to them. The simple lesson: keep moving forward, not back, throughout the event.

Anticipating trouble is just misplaced focus. Building negative feelings about a challenge that might occur, especially a worst-possible scenario, makes you far less capable of staying in the moment and performing at full power. In talking about the different risk quotient in employees, Microsoft executive Mark Angiulo observes that when people are scared they tend to underperform. Positive thinking yields positive results. It's not a coincidence. Mike sees part of being a leader as making his team feel comfortable with risks, and he does so by sharing insights like this: "The perception that people have of risk is generally flawed. If you ask most business leaders to plot the highest and lowest points for the industry three years out, most people will create a funnel of possibilities with only about a third in the range of actual likelihood. You can worry about the risks forever, but that doesn't make sense unless you understand the risks."

In short, success is affected enormously by your mind-set. You don't want to have to rely on someone else to create your success. Say to yourself: I'm going to have competition. I'm going to have to deal with limited capital. Acknowledge the sun might be in your eyes, is in your eyes, and will probably be in your eyes at some later point, and then succeed anyway instead of making yourself a victim of circumstances.

———————

There will be challenges, setbacks, and obstacles, and you should not pretend they won't exist. But don't let them set your agenda. Stay focused on the goal and let that set your agenda. Dealing with them is part of your success.

CHAPTER 16

Let Your Horse Read You:

Influence Others with Your Behaviors and Results

METRICSTREAM CEO SHELLYE Archambeau learned a lot about leadership by competing in dressage, a precision sport that cultivates a horse's ability for gymnastic maneuvers with minimal input from the rider: "If you're nervous, the horse is nervous. If you're not confident, the horse is not confident either. The horse can sense how you feel, so how you present yourself is a predictor of what the result is going to be."

In business, when you're a leader, people in your environment are more attuned to you than to others in certain key ways. They sense the slightest change in personality, demeanor, and mood. They are on to your "tells," as a cardplayer would say. It is the body language that reveals your true message regardless of what you say. If you show fear, your team is affected by that. When things are stressful and uncertain, they look to you to be sure things will be all right. Your attitude is always showing.

Once I was walking to a meeting room with a CEO when he said, "I really have to watch what I say. A few days ago I was walking down this hall and offhandedly said, 'Gee, this would look better with a new coat of paint.' The next day, I noticed it had been painted."

Lead by Persuasion, Not Fear

After earning her undergraduate business degree from the Wharton School, Shellye started in sales at IBM for a simple, goal-directed reason: the CEOs of the company had all started out in sales. She quickly noticed other success factors come into play, particularly the ability to speak publicly. The people who could present well seemed to have a generally higher level of achievement and prominence than the silent types. So at 21 she joined Toastmasters, which gave her a venue to practice. Her new skill contributed to a growing self-awareness as well as the impact she could have on others.

In my coaching I always tell people that presentation skills are not only a success factor in deal making, but also one of the best opportunities you have for your colleagues to become more aware of your talents and abilities than they currently are. There is an element of constructive and appropriate self-promotion.

The twin powers of presentation and persuasion allow leadership to take shape once it bubbles to the surface. During those days at IBM, Shellye's team faced a crossroads. They had invested a lot of time in developing a dramatic expansion plan for their operation and believed firmly in the bottom-line results it would yield. It required a substantial increase in budget. The boss went to his boss and pitched the project. Immediately afterward he came to the area where the team had gathered and depressed everyone with the body language and attitude of failure. When he opened his mouth with the bad news and apology, the mood only got worse.

"Wait a minute, guys!" Shellye told them. "All the company said was that we don't have the dollars and resources right this second to take on this ambitious expansion." She reminded them that they still had a solid budget, even though it was only 60 percent of what they wanted.

Her message was like a wind blowing their self-sabotaging mood out the door. The power of persuasion gets people to look at the situation for what it is: don't make it worse; make it better.

And for Shellye it reinforced the point that, no matter what title she held, she could be a leader. She became the leader of the group, even though she wasn't the titled, official leader.

Her experience early on, as well as through the years, substantiates words of wisdom from Bill Baker, polar explorer and president emeritus of Educational Broadcasting Corporation: "Leading with fear works only in the short term. It leads to defections and not receiving honest feedback." In contrast, leading by persuasion instills loyalty and promotes honesty.

Skier Kirill Tatarinov often has a slightly different challenge in terms of leading and influencing people in his role as corporate vice president of Microsoft Business Solutions at Microsoft Corp. Kirill works with an enormous group of partners, so they are people whose behavior and motivations he needs to affect but over whom he has no direct authority. His success formula is twofold: (1) Be thoughtful of what's driving them. What is their core interest? (2) Be thoughtful of how to balance your interest with theirs.

Dr. Bill Baker, president emeritus of Educational Broadcasting Corporation, at the North Pole

Never Forget That Authenticity Is Powerful; Exhibit It by Performing

Your performance sets the pace and the standards for your colleagues. They notice what you do. You can get deferential treatment from people if you can influence their compensation and day-to-day job responsibilities, but true authority means earning responsiveness through your actions. At that point commitment to working with you and toward mutual goals gives the deferential behavior meaning. You not only are a leader but also deserve to be a leader.

People will be loyal to the organization and to you, and that will not happen with someone who exercises authority just because of having the ability to sign paychecks. Being an effective boss is all about persuasion and inspiration.

Just Do It If You Want Others to Do It Too

The single most common element among all the people we have interviewed is that they are tremendously competitive. As a corollary, they deliberately engage their talents to promote self-improvement because they realize that the better they are, the more competitive they will be.

As leaders they tend to take great pride in asserting they would never ask anyone to do something they wouldn't do. The implication in that statement would be that there is something they couldn't do if they wanted to—and that's unacceptable to an innately competitive person. These are the generals who lead from the front.

When Olympic bobsledder Gord Woolley went into the print business, he wanted to make money. He found out that an essential part of achieving that goal occasionally meant taking off his boss hat, rolling up his sleeves, and assembling product in the warehouse.

When he was a university student, Gord worked as a laborer in a paper mill. After graduating, his father pushed him toward sales. For three years he sold paper to the printers. As his competitive bobsledding activities revved up, his confidence grew. He came back from the Olympics in 1984 and told his boss, who had been most accommodating all through the years that Gord took time off to train, "Thank you for everything, but I have to tell you: after all these years of selling paper to the printers, I know that the print guys make a lot more money than the paper guy."

After landing a job in the print industry, he struck out on his own and early on landed a deal that was the foundation of his success: all of the banners, posters, and other material for new promotions at McDonald's restaurants in Canada. Great work, but often labor intensive, so if the labor calls in sick and temps don't show up, the boss's hands are suddenly more useful than his brain. And not just for an hour, but sometimes for a whole day or more.

The guy with the corner office has got to be willing to do whatever it takes to succeed if everyone else in the company is expected to give 100 percent.

CHAPTER 17

Help Them to Summit with You:

Create Ways for People to Achieve More as Part of the Team than by Going It Alone

PRESTON CLINE, WILDERNESS athlete and associate director of the Wharton Leadership Ventures program, helps tests the leadership capabilities of M.B.A. students by putting them in positions where the consequences of their actions are extreme and immediate—on some of the world's highest mountains. Mountaineer Chris Warner, who has gone to the top of these high peaks around the world more than 150 times, has developed an experiential program with Preston for Wharton's M.B.A. students that holds people accountable to what their intentions are as well as their actions.

Preston's research is on human interaction with uncertainty, and the program Chris conducts helps him study what the students' fallback mechanisms are: fight, flight, or freeze. In looking at high-performance teams like those on the expeditions and monitoring how they perform, he helps the students understand whether or not their fallback mechanisms are sustainable.

Chris Warner, founder of Earth Treks, Inc., on the 12th highest peak in the world, 26,400-foot Broad Peak, on the border of Pakistan and China
Tao Franken, 2005

Preston says, "Everyone can talk about getting 100 percent of the people to the top of the mountain. But the program here is different. These are highly competitive M.B.A. students who all want to get to the top. There are always people who don't have the stamina to push on. They can't breathe. They have a headache. The inclination of the others is to keeping moving to the top and leave the slower climbers behind. Chris then says, 'This is the point in your whole life when decisions truly matter. This is the point where the easy solution is to let them go.'"

Preston is careful to point out that this isn't a situation in which bringing someone along presents safety issues. It's just a matter of someone going a little slower. This is about a person who has skills to bring to the team, but endurance isn't one of them. So Chris is there offering the "voice from above," asking them, "is leaving this person behind really the decision you want to make? What are the longer-term consequences in your life of making a decision like this—a decision that serves your selfish needs but not the needs of the team?"

Those are moments that people never forget.

Act on the Truth That We All Aspire to Be Part of Something Greater than Ourselves

The most memorable experiences in life are commonly the ones in which you're part of something greater than you could have ever achieved on your own. Sports team, military, family, community, company—think of all of the truly high points in your life and then consider the role that other people played in making them so extraordinary. When your high school basketball team wins the state championship, that victory belongs to you as player or even as a die-hard fan. When your volunteer organization raises enough money for a new ambulance in town, every time you see it speeding toward the scene of an accident, you know that a piece of your talent and time put that vehicle on the road.

There's a sense of transcendence. The accomplishment is not something you could have done alone, and that is precisely what gives it such weight in your life. You connected effectively with other people and made a noteworthy thing happen.

The dynamic in which hardened individualists come together to perform as a team must involve this sense of "the whole being greater than the parts" or there won't be a "whole." Skydiving world records provide a perfect example of the challenge of coordinating the efforts of hundreds of such people. Imagine asking splinters to form a two-by-four. These sharp shards of ego have to be convinced that coming together is a desirable thing and that subordinating personal interests for the good of a team will feel amazing.

There is always a point in the attempts when it becomes apparent that this transition to group-think and group-achievement will either happen or not happen.

Interestingly, as soon as a group of high-performance skydivers like this actually builds a world-record formation, they lapse back into their individualistic natures. I have been part of a couple of world records in which, after we succeeded, we attempted to build even bigger formations to break the record we had just set. It never worked. By that time the focus on and commitment to being a team had dissipated.

Attorneys are not naturally team oriented either, so Pearl Law Group founder Julie Pearl's business model for her firm seems unnatural to them.

She underlines the necessity of team problem solving with policies like this: unless a client's request brings a moral or ethical issue into play, you cannot tell a client no on behalf of the firm. Among other contrarian actions, Julie did not like the fact that attorneys bill on an hourly basis because she felt it was a conflict of interest, so her firm runs counter to the industry standard by billing on a fixed-fee basis.

To determine whether a prospective member of the staff will fit in, she listens for "we" rather than "I" during the interview process. Too much "I did this" rather than "We did this" means that person will not be joining the firm. A "team of attorneys" sounds a bit like an oxymoron, but this element of the screening process helps to make it more of a realistic possibility.

This is not about doing something differently; it's about how you position the opportunities. Joining the law firm or showing up for a world-record attempt will incite team spirit among individualists as long as the prospect of achieving something great infects everyone's energy.

Sustaining that spirit in business offers greater challenges than in sky-diving or mountain climbing, for example, because you want the team to stay together for an extended period of time. With few exceptions, expedition climbs cannot be done alone. The expedition therefore creates a sense of team-building urgency because the team exists solely for the purpose of summiting a particular mountain; it will not stay together forever.

Businesses can learn from this. Goal clarity for each project, with benchmarks that can be celebrated along the way, will renew the team's energy and reinforce the reasons for acting like they belong together.

Julie Pearl's law firm handles immigration law exclusively. She had a team assigned to get people from China to Costa Rica, but they had to do it very quickly—a goal complicated by the fact that Costa Rica had just opened a consulate in China and didn't have a lot of systems in place yet. She thought of the challenge as a lot like her scuba diving: there's only a finite amount of air in your tanks, so there's only so much bottom time you can manage. Knowing that, you have to figure out a way to meet your objective for the dive. The team succeeded through meticulous planning, persistence, and creativity. The sense of urgency in getting the job done was real, and it provided fuel for moving forward hour by hour.

Sell a Vision

The hardest part of selling a vision is the physicality. You can prepare a sound plan and present it with conviction, thereby capturing the mental and emotional investment you've made in the project. But until you have done something tangible to demonstrate commitment, your vision is still only a dream to other people.

Polar explorer Bill Baker believes that a fundamental skill in building a successful business or athletic venture is selling your vision. In his experience as head of Educational Broadcasting, he had to convince donors, as well as business associates, to invest resources in the vision. Their reward would be public television, which they and many others could enjoy. In his precedent-setting North and South Pole expeditions, he also had to convince donors who would never personally experience the results to invest in his vision. What they would get is the satisfaction of supporting a journalist's adventure to the poles, that is, a trek so well documented that many people could share in the adventure.

He sees the two activities as being extremely similar in nature in terms of mechanics too: "Exploration is like business. It consists of the funding, the logistics, and the staffing."

Getting buy-in from people is all in the packaging and positioning. They must perceive your unique vision as an inspiring accomplishment and participation in the effort as a path to facilitating their own professional and personal goals. Bill says that the way you recruit high achievers is by "showing them that they can achieve more by being on your team than by functioning alone or being on another team." That makes them care about the effort as much as the vision.

The way Bill describes organizational relationships makes them sound like a dovetail joint, which is the image I use in my executive education sessions—in fact, I consider it an essential concept. In the same way that sections of wood can interlock to create a strong joint, it is possible to mate the goals and purposes of employees with those of an organization.

Build rapport with your employees so that you can identify what their personal goals are. You are then in a position to ascertain where they align with those of the organization. As someone responsible for conducting the activities of a team, keep in mind that if you can help people achieve their goals while simultaneously achieving those of the organization, you end up with more committed and loyal employees. The process of doing this relies on interpersonal relationships and not mechanics, so don't think you can get the same kind of usable information out of a survey conducted by your human resources department.

The premise of forging dovetail joints in an organization might be best depicted in a Venn diagram, where the circles' intersection represents the opportunity to engage the person at a higher level. The intersection is the area where personal and organizational aims overlap. Here is an example of how that might work: You decide you want your company to establish a beachhead in China. At a company gathering last year you had a conversation with an employee who happened to mention she was taking Chinese language and cooking lessons. Even though she works in a different department, you may be well served to engage her interest in Chinese culture by involving her in the China initiative to dovetail the two interests.

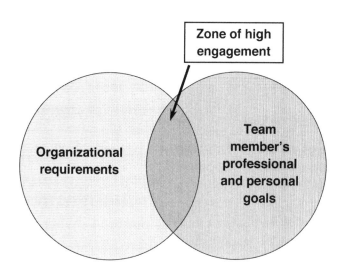

Dovetailing — Aligning organizational needs
with a team member's aspirations

Regardless of what the elements of convergence are, the results of discovering and acting on them can be tremendous engagement and tremendous loyalty. You feed a deeply held desire to be a part of something grand. Go back to the discussion in Chapter 13 of how to build a Magnetic Culture; note that one of the points is "provide desired job content." Dovetailing is a way to do it.

CHAPTER 18

Use Superior Judgment to Avoid Using Superior Skills:

Maintain Situational Awareness

AEROBATIC PILOT MIKE Angiulo likes to quote astronaut Frank Borman in talking about preparing for a good outcome despite risk: "A superior pilot uses his superior judgment to avoid using his superior skills." Properly executed, aerobatic flying is not exciting, he says, and that assertion tracks with what I would say about skydiving and what many other extreme athletes have said about their potentially dangerous athletic activities: "You manage the risk in advance. You drill and you train for various situations, but not only do they not happen, but you don't worry about them."

His comment points precisely to the value of cultivating situational awareness.

Fellow Microsoft executive Kirill Tatarinov draws from his competitive skiing experience in capturing a variation on the same lesson: you have to think about the course and choose the path that will get you to the finish line in the shortest amount of time. Sometimes you know full well that that

163

path may not be a straight line because of the obstacles and bumps. You want to get as close as possible to the straight line, but don't obsess on it.

It is an insight that has many variations, but the fundamental lesson is to make decisions based on a keen and specific attentiveness to your environment.

The companion question to why people take large risks in athletic activities is "how," and one of the key answers is that over time extreme sports improve situational awareness. By doing them again and again, climbers, skydivers, skiers, scuba divers—all types of athletes in high-risk situations— get better at choosing when to pull back and when to push forward.

This is one of the critical lessons learned by participants in the Wharton Leadership Ventures program. By taking on major mountains like Cotapaxi in Ecuador and Kilimanjaro in Tanzania, program leaders like Preston Cline see what the default response is for these high-performance M.B.A. students when they are faced with decision making that has immediate and serious consequences. Despite their intelligence and drive, can they process enough information about their surroundings to make sound choices?

The two-part challenge in maintaining situational awareness is questioning assumptions and staying aware of what's going on.

Continually Question the Status Quo

Part of being a visionary is being willing to question the status quo, to ask the healthy and provocative questions about how things can be done better. This is not a matter of taking a contrarian position just for the sake of thinking differently, but rather of not going into a stupor and making a failed assumption that what's taking place today will be taking place tomorrow. It is thinking that challenges productively. If people in the company have been making decisions and taking initiatives based on certain suppositions, it's important to ask whether those notions that were valid last week are valid today. That's part of the process of maintaining situational awareness. You will kill your business if you do not have it.

Deidre Paknad laughs when people ask her what her five-year plan is. She tells them there is no possibility of developing a five-year plan to operate effectively in the records-management software industry because of the rapid change. She considers her primary job using her change radar to see what's coming in terms of products, services, and customer needs and adjusting plans accordingly.

Be Heads-Up and Try to Look Around the Corner

As pilot and CAE executive Jeff Roberts points out, flying involves making sure you have an intimate understanding of the environment and all the factors around you, anticipating and trying to manipulate those factors to a successful conclusion, and being cognizant of the risks or potential risks you might encounter. And, as with business, you can never have enough information and you will never have all the information. One of the skills that both executives and pilots must develop is the mental organization to deal with whatever facts are available and then figure out, as you go along,

Mike Angiulo, competitive aerobatics pilot and Microsoft Corporation's general manager of the Microsoft Project business unit

Russell Williams

when you have enough information to make a decision that has a high likelihood of being the right decision.

Jeff calls it the skill of "looking around the corner."

"Every decent pilot is always trying to stay out in front of the airplane. I try to do the same thing in business. If I'm going 600 miles an hour in an airplane, I can't decide at the last minute that I'm going to try to land at a place that's 10 miles ahead if I'm at 40,000 feet. I decide 100 miles ahead so I can take the steps to land at the airport safely. Same thing in business. You have to be able to look around the corner at what's happening in the market, what's going on with your employees, your competitors, and try to take steps in advance of what's coming next."

The need for situational awareness is one reason trade shows will never die. They are intelligence environments as much as anything else. Executives go primarily to see what their competitors are doing. (How many times have you flipped your badge to the back side so a competitor wouldn't see what color stripe you have on your name tag?) There are books and courses devoted to the subjects of what to wear, how to question, and how to organize observations to gather competitive intelligence at trade shows—it's all the fine points of honing situational awareness.

Situational awareness involves everything from intangibles like shifts in market trends to the body language of people with whom you're negotiating a deal. The key to applying your skill is knowing what signs and signals have meaning in the particular circumstance. Discussions in Part 3, "Team Excellence," will help you refine your sense of what those are.

CHAPTER 19

Rush to the Medal Stand:

Celebrate Your Victories

IN SPORTS THERE is a moment when either you cross the finish line first or someone else wins. You summit, or you don't reach the top. You complete the formation or end your skydive having failed to do so. In all cases you have some measure of success by merely surviving the experience.

You also have a defined sense of progress in many extreme sports. CAE's group president Jeff Roberts, a former aerobatics pilot, finds that part of the satisfaction of flying is that there is a beginning, a middle, and an end.

Many of our athlete-executives said that in their business lives they missed those clearly defined steps toward success along with the definite moments of victory. They sought ways to replicate them to whatever extent was reasonable as a way of energizing their teams and keeping their focus on outcomes.

They wanted to find ways to recognize genuine successes and celebrate them in ways that are appropriate for the business and the team. Many of them said they also wanted to have fun when commemorating business victories of any magnitude.

From left to right: Kirby Best, former CEO of Ingram Lightning Source, and Gordon Woolley, president of Jessam Communications, with teammates Greg Alford and David Leuty at the 1983 World Championships in Lake Placid

Make the Celebrations Fact Based

For the celebration to be anything more than an ice-cream social, where people roll their eyes and wonder why some company executive decided to humor them, the reason for the reward must have substance.

Mere completion of a project or just reaching the end of a quarter without losing your shirts is not a good reason for a party or gift certificates to the wine store.

Maryann worked for an organization that scheduled celebrations. Once a year everyone trudged off to the company picnic and pretended to enjoy eating potato salad with people from other departments. Once a month the entire staff of 40 got together to celebrate employee birthdays and corporate victories that had occurred in the previous month. As they shuffled down the hall to the big meeting room, staff members looked at each other and sighed, "Oh, boy—cake."

In business it can be hard to know when to celebrate. A company may go for extended periods without a definable success unless it operates in a world of deal making, such as real estate, investment banking, or any area of sales. Hopefully, there will be little things every day that elicit remarks like "That worked out well." And then there are the "wow" moments, when some group of employees or maybe the whole company says, "Wow, we truly excelled!"

The leader of an organization, or a division, needs to sort these moments out in terms of importance. The chief executives will often see things, good and bad, that people in the trenches haven't observed. The view from above gives senior executives an opportunity to see how the puzzle pieces have come together and created an outcome worth commemorating. It should also reveal when lots of pieces are missing. The people in the body design division of a car manufacturer may feel as though they should have a party because their new model earned rave reviews. But those in an R&D division don't really deserve a party quite yet—or so some people might think—because they have not yet managed to design a car engine that runs on water. They may not have an unqualified success for 10 years. Does that mean they have nothing to celebrate?

The challenge for both the person on top and the division heads is to determine when and how to celebrate successes so they are based in real, measurable accomplishments. The method of establishing those laudable outcomes will likely vary a great deal from department to department. The person on top looks at the big picture and may conclude that the new body design, combined with the great PR generated by the work of the R&D division, provides enough substance to warrant a company-wide celebration. The R&D division head may see that the work of her team has led to immediate improvements in engine efficiency, even though they have not reached their ultimate goal. Celebrate that.

Match Incentives to Desired Behavior

The issue of what constitutes an appropriate reward or celebration plagues a lot of executives. It doesn't have to be money. It doesn't have to be a Hawaiian getaway for the family. I used to keep gift certificates for the nearby ice cream and cookie stores in my desk as a quick "thanks for the extra effort."

People appreciated the immediate gratification of running next door and picking up freshly baked cookies. Something like that works well for the small stuff that is still a cut above what's required for the job. Kirby Best would hand out Popsicles for reaching sales thresholds. He also threw a Canadian wet T-shirt contest—despite the fervent protests of his legal and HR departments—for his team on one occasion to celebrate a success. (I had to ask what that was too. The first one to thaw out the frozen T-shirt and put it on got a prize.) In short, the reward doesn't have to be large, but it should match both the spirit and the corporate value of the accomplishment.

A corollary issue relates to incentives, which may be tied to accomplishments but often are tied to expectations. Be careful what you incentivize, because you will get it.

One of my colleagues served as a consultant to a Silicon Valley company that provided an incentive trip for its entire marketing and public relations team. They went to the wine country for diversity training so they would improve their relationships with colleagues and communications with a diverse public about the company's consumer products. Three fabulous days later, they had people sowing the seeds of the next trip. Now that they had this diversity thing down, maybe they could make a case for a trip to help understand the government market better. Washington, D.C., in late spring would be nice. Was this gracious reward tied to any accomplishment? No. While it likely assisted morale, it did not serve as performance recognition.

The important thing is that the reward corresponds to the level of accomplishment, reinforces a message about the mission, and be timed to be meaningful.

Recognize Successes Immediately After They Occur

Provide the bonus, party, or gift certificate as soon after the accomplishment as possible.

Companies make a huge mistake when they dangle incentive compensation before employees and then wait months, or even a year, to deliver on the promised reward. The behavior they are trying to reward and reinforce can easily fade in that time, with employees receiving a bonus or vacation package long after they may have slumped into ordinary performance.

The relationship to the behavior that the company is trying to encourage is lost.

Reward the Intelligent Risk Takers, Even When They Fail

Similarly, the company Maryann worked for that had the planned parties corrupted the correlation between performance and reward by scheduling celebratory events once a month and in the summer "no matter what."

The celebrations with little or no value are the arbitrary ones, those that reward people who don't deserve it, and those that honor people for simply doing the job they were hired to do.

All of these bad choices have a common thread: cowardice. The person in charge of the incentive/reward program, whatever form it takes, has decided that no one should be left out because that might hurt someone's feelings or it would be bad for overall morale. Baloney. Executive after executive we interviewed affirmed the belief that doling out gifts to employees who do not deserve them is as productive as burning your profits in a George Foreman Grill. You can cook a few burgers on it, but you won't be able to buy any more grills.

You do have to be prepared for the management challenge of a disgruntled employee, however. By not giving an underperformer a bonus, are you passively trying to drive the person out of the organization, or would you prefer to invest the bonus money in retraining or coaching for the employee? If it's the latter, state your intention and invite a response; see how much buy-in you get. If it's the former, then help the person find a new environment more quickly by firing him.

Give Yourself a Medal Too

"When you're done with a marathon, someone hands you a certificate that says, 'Congratulations, you're done!' When you're the boss and you close a deal, no one hands you a certificate that says, 'Congratulations, you're done!' In fact, you're not done. You're just starting." There are a couple of good lessons in what Dennis Sponer is saying here, but one of them is a reminder that you can't forget to reward yourself. Yes, when you close a deal you are just starting, but take a minute to open your ears and let your employees and colleagues congratulate you. And give yourself a Popsicle.

Gord Woolley, Canadian Olympic bobsled team member and founder and president of Jessam Communications, always likes to look for places where he can declare he is winning, just as he did in his bobsledding days. He celebrates a new order, a new client, or any other quantifiable victory. To him, it's like saying, "We won the meet." That's not the same as taking the gold, but it represents the possibility of taking the gold.

TEAM EXCELLENCE

CHAPTER 20

Add 10 Feet to Your Jump:

Insist on Goal Clarity

THE PART 2 lessons set you up to capitalize on the full potential of your team. The Part 3 lessons will fully engage you with your team to push toward new heights.

When waterskiing champion Camille Duvall-Hero's father sat her down to make her goals for the following year, he talked in terms of metrics. It reflected his orientation as an engineer. She would write down things like "improve my slalom score by three buoys" or "add 10 feet to my jump."

While metrics do not work for all kinds of goals, Camille's dad captured the essence of goal clarity: Be explicit. As a corollary, state the goal in a way that people not only get it but want to get it. Camille, who already held the world record for jumping, took a goal like adding 10 feet to her jump and completed the thought with "to set a new world record."

Make Sure Everyone Is Clear on the Goal

At its worst, goal setting can be as pernicious an exercise as marriage might be for those with multiple divorces in their history. Too often what is missing is the sense of optimism that magnetically draws people toward a sense of success. Sometimes the harm is that the result of the process seems innocuous. People think, "We're just going to sell the same burgers we sold today, so who cares about some stupid company goal?"

Goals need to affect people on two levels. Typically, company executives consider market conditions, performance of the competition, and corporate resources relative to their competitors' in establishing financial goals for the quarter, the year, and years beyond. That's only half the picture. Internal factors—the talents, skills, and commitment of people who must try to achieve corporate goals—determine what the company can achieve. Those factors, therefore, need to be considered in goal setting.

The clarity of the goal is how well it invites each individual to participate in achieving it.

Remember That Goal Clarity Will Empower Your Team to Make Good Decisions

Ideally you want everyone in the organization to be able to tell you what the goal is—and to have that one-line response be on the tips of customers' and media tongues as well. To the extent that message has been absorbed within the organization, the decision-making process becomes that much simpler at every level of the company. Guiding every choice is the question "Does this move us closer to the goal or further away from it?" As a result,

Author and world-record skydiver Jim McCormick enjoying a rare solo jump on a winter day in the skies above Colorado

fewer decisions must be escalated; people at every level have some real power in making choices because they understand what the organization aims to achieve. The result is an agile organization. People throughout have a strong sense of which direction to go and what to avoid. Unlike the preponderance of corporate mission statements, which blah-blah-blather on in industry-speak, Southwest Airlines states simply: "The mission of Southwest Airlines is dedication to the highest quality of Customer Service delivered with a sense of warmth, friendliness, individual pride, and Company Spirit." If anyone on staff cannot remember that—remembering being fundamental to living the message—I would be shocked.

One of the signs of maturity you see in a world-record effort is that the goal-centered methodologies of hundreds of individual people start to gel. People in different sections of the large formation begin to work on their

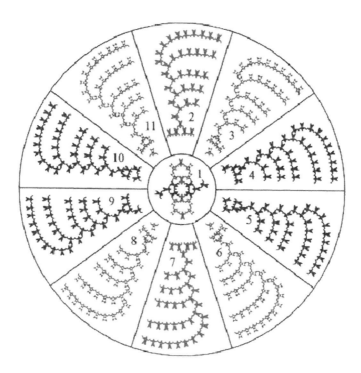

World-record 400-way skydiving formation showing 10 sectors and a base in the center. Jim was in sector 9.

recurring problems in their area on their own; for purposes of this discussion, I'll focus on the 400-person world-record skydiving formation we did in Thailand in 2006.

Small groups of people soon determined how to coordinate their moves better without involving their sector captains. They looked at the traffic patterns they faced and ways they could help each other dock on the formation efficiently. That level of cooperation brings a higher likelihood of success than when people try to drive toward the goal individually.

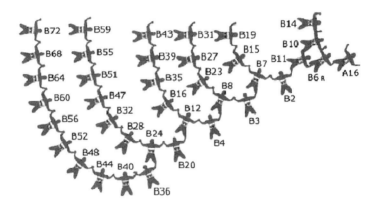

Sector diagram showing each skydiver. Jim's slot was B15.

Paradoxically, each sector made complexity look simple. This illustration of one sector—my slot was B15—may help you imagine how row after row would need to build. Even though it is a single individual who joins one row to the next (such as B2, B3, and B4), that person cannot possibly do his or her job unless the entire row is flying toward the center.

Now increase the complexity level of a large-formation skydive in a different way—not by adding people but by asking those people to fly formations that had never been tried before. That's what we did in building formations for Honda's "Difficult Is Worth Doing" ad campaign. A formation looking like a coil spring topped the list of challenges. Forty-five people flew together to form a four-loop configuration, which would have been less difficult if the pattern had not required half of the people to be looking away from the center. This is a little like asking drivers to speed into their spaces in a parking lot simultaneously, with half of them backing in while the other half are moving forward.

What I suggested—and having a background in engineering may have helped here—was that we take our positions facing inward, and then those people who need to be face out should turn outward, one at a time, so that each section of the loop would take shape sequentially. By doing that, each person could keep an eye on the center until it was time to turn away. Each person would therefore be steady in the designated direction before the turning person took a grip.

There is an innate sense of urgency in this situation because you are falling toward the earth at 120 miles an hour, and that factor is what drove people to make mistakes initially. In addition, this team consisted of some of the best skydivers in the world, all wanting to do it perfectly the first time. We also knew that each jump was expensive—multiple planes, free-fall cameramen shooting film, and ground support. Planning the turns sequentially in the time allotted gave us the system to accomplish the job with a good margin of safe working time built in. We were immediately successful with this approach.

Some business goals involve this kind of very real time sensitivity due to market pressures. Goal clarity makes it possible for a subgroup of the team—just like our subgroup of the Honda ad team—to collaborate without getting anyone in authority involved and to solve problems independently to make progress. Being clear on the goal empowered decision making and agility.

For this to work optimally, of course, the team must be composed of people who have a good sense of their own abilities and limitations. When we built the 400-way world record, as the team was forming, months in advance of the attempts in Thailand, we got an e-mail from our sector captain with the illustration included here. His question: Where do you want to be in the sector? You could specify one specific slot or give him a range, but the choice was based on where each of us felt we would perform best. The process drew on our self-awareness at the same time as it gave us a role in the process that took us above that of worker bees and into the realm of decision makers.

The efficiencies associated with fewer role changes on site could not be underestimated—not to mention the public relations value. Our team demonstrated to our royal Thai sponsors that we took this exercise very seriously and approached it professionally. The benefit of decision-making input from multiple, qualified sources—rather than just a couple of organizers—showed up in commitment, attitude, and performance.

Establish Personal Goals While Honoring Organizational Goals

Personal coach Kristen Ulmer counsels executives to be true to their innate talents and passion and to allow their personal goal to evolve. That evolving goal, as vital as it is to self-awareness, is something they may have to keep to themselves, though. A board of directors may get uneasy thinking that the CEO has a goal of evolving as he makes major financial decisions.

Kirby Best has an approach that is both consistent with Kristen's Zen-based guidance (see Chapter 8) and appropriate for profit-directed boards of directors. One of the lessons from his competitive days that he had to unlearn relates to setting goals to achieve unparalleled performance. His inner voice told him the only goals he could have were superlatives like number one, gold medal, and fastest. In the corporate environment, he had to learn to promise *less* than he felt he and his team were capable of achieving. In good conscience, how could he underpromise and overdeliver? How could he declare, as his gut told him to, that he would be the best—that he would bring in $1 billion—when he knew that promising $500 million and bringing in $750 million would make him look better?

The way he handled it was to have public goals and private goals. The team would set the goal that they would live by internally, and then there would be the goal that they would articulate for the rest of the company and the board of directors. It was not an insignificant goal by any means since the owner of the company and the board always pressed them to make the goal that met their financial needs. "We just set ours higher," says Kirby.

Establish a private goal consistent with your desire to reach the stars and you will easily achieve the public goal of reaching the moon.

CHAPTER 21

Think the Rush; Don't Just Feel It:

See Risk as a Tool, Not a Threat

DONE WELL, RISK taking is the artful convergence of opportunity, talents, and resources. Done in a disciplined and intelligent manner, risk taking is a powerful tool.

Mark Richey unequivocally attributes his success to the ability to go to the edge: "We built our business on risk taking. I started with nothing. I had a $300 apartment in Waltham, Massachusetts, with a basement millwork shop. I employ over a hundred people now. We do over $20 million in volume a year." He took on jobs that were "too big" for the company and could have put him out of business at any moment, but his intelligent risk taking moved in tandem with his own persistence, as well as the contributions of his wife and team, who seemed to have the same kind of appetite for risk as Mark.

Determine Your Risk Quotient

Mark is clearly well matched with his team in terms of a predilection for risk taking. But how do you screen yourself, as well as other people, for this ability?

You have heard of IQ, or intelligence quotient, and EQ, or emotional quotient. I add RQ, or risk quotient, to that collection of personal evaluators.

Each person has a natural level of risk, and when you go beyond it, you feel uncomfortable. That threshold is the RQ. It is an indication of your risk inclination over a broad range of risk types: physical, career, financial, social, intellectual, creative, relationship, emotional, and spiritual. Think of your RQ as a number between 1 and 10, with 1 being very risk averse and 10 being very risk inclined. The risk inclination research that I've done over time has shown that men have an average RQ of 6.7 on a scale of 1 to 10, and women have an average of 6.4. If you'd like to determine yours, go to wwwtakerisks.com/tools and take the free personal risk profile.

RQ is a concept used in investing and portfolio theory as an indication of an investor's risk tolerance. It also surfaces in assessing environmental issues, supply chain management, and the political stability of countries. Using it to discuss personal excellence or team leadership is a new application, but it's certainly valid given the way that the athlete-executives in this book keep circling back to intelligent risk taking as a key success factor.

Risking less than your RQ makes you feel like you're not challenging yourself enough; risking beyond your RQ makes you feel uncomfortable.

Your RQ is another way of framing the concept of comfort zone, that area where you function with relative ease. Going outside generally provokes inconsistent performance. The surge in fear causes your brain to lose some cognitive function while your emotional responses rise up. As Mike Angiulo expresses it: "Risk can make people scared, and when they are scared, they can underperform. The goal is to mitigate the risk until it is not affecting your decision making."

When you think of your RQ as a point on a line between two extremes—with risk averse on the far left and risk inclined on the far right—everything to the left of the RQ point is your comfort zone. What the people in this book have done through various experiences and decisions is to move that point farther and farther to the right to expand their comfort zone beyond what most people see as normal.

As leaders, the people in this book have very similar approaches in the way they help people around them increase their risk quotient. The fundamental principle involves three things:

- Incremental shifts toward greater risk taking
- Reality checks about the potential outcomes, good and bad
- Rewards consistent with the effort

The principle of incremental growth is the same one that all of these athletes have used to become competitive, accomplish record-breaking feats, and gain world-class status. They started moving in the direction of excellence and just kept moving there, step-by-step. No one was born with the ability to climb K2. So, if a person on your team has an enormous fear of making a presentation to a room of 200 people, don't start with 200 people. Start him out with five friendly bodies in a situation where it doesn't matter. Let him build up to 10.

The whole time you are working through incremental gains, you must count on mentors and coaches to provide reality checks. When you fear risk, you have a sense that if you do x, then y could happen, and that spells catastrophe. That fear can cause you to do whatever it takes to make sure that never happens—which means you never do x. Set up your incremental growth in intelligent risk taking so the risk is tolerable at the same time it tests underlying assumptions.

Attorney Paul Geller, member of the executive committee of Coughlin Stoia

Finally, as I've said in many other places in this book, make sure rewards go to those who attempt greatness, not just those who attempt it and succeed.

Know the Difference Between Intelligent Risks and Fatal Risks

Aerobatic pilot Mike Angiulo draws a dramatic distinction between the kind of risk in aviation or business that gets your heart racing with victory and one that is heart stopping—for good. This is the difference between an adrenaline rush, which slams you into equal amounts of uncertainty and thrill, and a competence rush, which gives you instant cause for celebrating your balance of risk taking and judgment.

Mike began his career with a greater focus on the former. With his future wife as his fellow outlaw, he would paraglide off high points in the national park, where it is illegal to do it. They would drive to various "scenic overlooks," which generally feature a gorgeous view and a steep cliff. His wife would ease the car closest to the cliff, stand on top of the car holding up Mike's paraglider, and he would go charging down the hill, hoping to float down to a spot where she could pick him up later.

Maturity, which could have happened only because he survived his adrenaline rush days, led to a different approach to adventure flying. It became intelligent risk taking: "Once you have gotten to the point where you have spun your airplane in every attitude—upright, inverted, flat, accelerated—you know that your responses to recovery are immediate and automatic. You've maintained your airplane properly and done a thorough preflight; you know that you're healthy. The instant you roll into the box where you're diving down at maximum speed, you're pointed straight at the ground . . . it's like you're not flying an airplane; you're in a video game, surrounded by a cone of invulnerability because you've done everything you possibly could to mitigate the risks. You've convinced yourself the risks are manageable. You have confidence in your training. In that moment, you're free to perform. And set up to win.

"In business, if you have too much at risk, or you're outside your realm of competence and you know it, everything you do is with anxiety around the outcome or a certain amount of hesitation. And if you get too overconfident and think you can do it all, you become a smoking hole in just a matter of seconds."

Mountaineer and entrepreneur John Wilson learned this lesson early in life. A 23-year-old John was returning from the Philippines after serving in the Peace Corps. He bought a Honda 175 motorcycle and, starting in Singapore, went through 26 countries and 25,000 miles before he ended up in Philadelphia. That would be stupid for someone who had never done a major motorcycle trip before—unless you did it like John. Beyond doing geograph-

ical research, he read six books on motorcycling so that he could pick up the
best tips from others who had done extensive cycling. "Don't drive at night"
was one rule he found in those books that he adhered to throughout his year
on the road.

Later on, when he sought adventures on the world's greatest mountains,
he brought his sense of risk mitigation to every expedition. But the sensi-
bility he honed about taking risks is actually more preemptive than that.
"In mountaineering," he concludes, "you can select which risks you want to
take," and that is a key lesson he brings to business: don't just handle risk
well; choose your risks well.

Through the years I have met a lot of people who say, "You, skydive?!" to
me with equal parts fascination and criticism. I explain what most people
don't know: skydivers like me (and that is most of us) have a lot of ways
to pull the experience toward enjoyment and away from danger. There is a
huge difference between perceived and actual risk. Skydivers don't leave the
plane with a single parachute, a hope, and a prayer as many people think we
do. Our safety systems include the following elements of personal preparation and gear:

- Currency in the sport—that is, recent practice in doing skydives
- A reserve parachute that has been packed within the last 120 days by
  a professional certified by the U.S. Federal Aviation Administration
- An automatic activation device that has been properly maintained
  and inspected (This device triggers deployment of the reserve
  parachute if the main parachute has not been deployed by a prede-
  termined altitude and becomes critical if the skydiver has lost consciousness or altitude awareness.)
- An audible altimeter mounted in the helmet so that it sits adjacent to
  the ear and goes off at three preset altitudes and with three distinct
  tones (I set mine for 500 feet above the altitude where I intend to
  leave a formation to prepare for parachute deployment, at 1,000 feet
  above parachute deployment, and at minimum deployment altitude.)
- A digital altimeter that reads to accuracies of 100 feet in free fall and
  10 feet under canopy

Each element takes an activity with a lot of inherent danger and turns it into something that can be enjoyed. The risks of the sport do not vanish, but they become manageable and transform skydiving into an exercise in reasonable risk taking instead of something that only daredevils attempt.

Make Risk a Tool to Be Utilized, Not Minimized

Risk can kill you, but it can also yield life-changing innovations. How you regard risk is one of your defining characteristics and significantly influences most of your life choices. The genesis of your current relationship with risk—physical, social, emotional, or intellectual—is something that profoundly affected you. Reluctance to take physical risks might come from a concerned mom pulling you away from the metal slide or off the jungle gym when you were a toddler. Contrast that with the push toward risk and resourcefulness that Richard Branson's mom gave him when he was a kid: she opened the car door on the way to Grandma's and told him to make it the rest of the way himself.

Many of the athlete-executives we interviewed logged turning points in their life. These events set them off in a new direction and changed their lives. Some occurred over a period of time, like Paul Geller's getting addicted to martial arts movies when he was a kid. A highly successful litigator, founding partner of Coughlin Stoia, and Brazilian jujitsu champion, Paul begged his parents for lessons and has stuck with martial arts training and competition through adulthood, reaching great heights within the discipline. Some shifts occurred seemingly abruptly, as in Don Bell's case. In the mid-1970s he went to a vintage car race with his wife one week in San Francisco and the next week called her from Southern California at around 2:00 P.M.: "I'm leaving now. I'll be there tonight."

She said, "Why will it take you so long to get home?"

"I'm driving." And then he explained that he was pulling their new race car, a Porsche 550 Spider. He started vintage car racing immediately after that, and racing has been a key activity for him in the decades since.

Start looking for your own turning points in areas like education, career, location, and relationships. Differentiate between the ones that were imposed on you and the ones you determined yourself. Although someone influential may have introduced the athlete-executives in this book to their sports and their businesses, no one forced them to participate. As with the example of Richard Branson, they may have been predisposed to take risks because of something that a parent did, but no one said, "Richard, you have to fly across the ocean in a hot-air balloon."

Society at large contributes to the process of shaping your turning points, and while the athlete-executives certainly do not have identical backgrounds, many of them talked about growing up where it was cool to be a cowboy or "everybody" skied; their leap was taking the urge to extremes of achievement. Sharon Begley cited a study relevant to this in her October 27, 2008, *Newsweek* article "Math Is Hard, Barbie Said":

"How powerfully do social forces affect brain function? In a 2007 study, girls reminded of the girls-are-spatially-challenged stereotype did worse on a test of spatial ability than those who were not, and brain imaging showed why: they had higher activity in the [area of the brain that is] the site of negative emotions such as anger and sadness, and lower activity in high-order visual areas and complex working memory areas, found Maryjane Wraga of Smith College. Anxiety triggered by social forces had muted activity required for spatial reasoning."

Help Your Team Discover Their Tolerance for Risk

When Deidre Paknad first got to PSS Systems and pulled her team together, she asked them, if a start-up company were a sport, what sport would it be? The people who said "golf" soon found they had to reevaluate their relationship with the company. The answer she wanted was one that showed some understanding that the road ahead was steep, the water was deep, and there was a good chance they would get hurt. In other words, a start-up was an extreme sport. "The chance you could die exists, but if you survive, it will be the wildest, most satisfying ride you've ever been on," she told them. "And if that's not what you want, you're in the wrong place."

Critical self-reflection is a huge strength, and Deidre has found that the people who not only grasp but also look forward to the risk associated with a start-up tend to bring that asset to work with them every day. These are the people who may fail in the innovation phase but disclose the failure and point to ways that the knowledge might eventually lead to success. And they are rewarded, just like the people whose ideas lead to an immediate victory.

CHAPTER 22

Grapple like a Chess Master:

Manage Risk with Contingency Thinking

CONTINGENCY PLANNING MEANS you have options for action pre-planned so you can respond efficiently in a situation. Contingency thinking, in the way our athlete-executives talk about it, is a tool for responding to problems that may or may not occur and to reshape them quickly or mitigate their impact if they do occur. As John Wilson describes it, contingency thinking is "thought process that focuses on 'what-if?'" He recommends reading about others who have been through bad things and learning: you may wake up to good ideas about extricating yourself from disaster.

Paul Geller, founding partner of Coughlin Stoia, begged his parents to let him take jujitsu lessons when he was a kid. They probably thought he'd want astronaut school the next month, so they let him go. Paul stuck with it all through his teen years, college, and law school, but his passion didn't take shape until 1993, when he saw Rorion Gracie introduce Brazilian jujitsu to the world at the first Ultimate Fighting Championship.

Bob Stangarone, VP corporation communications of Cessna Aircraft Company, receiving his commercial pilot's license in 1969

In the Brazilian style, the focus is not on punching and kicking but on joint manipulation, chokes, strangulation, and other moves that, in the aggregate, constitute grappling.

Sounds rough—and it is—but Paul, ranked eighth nationwide in his age category and weight class, sees a major requirement as "having a chess mentality." Let's say his goal is to break someone's left arm. While he's on the ground, grappling with the opponent, he will position his body in a way that anticipates how the opponent is likely to counter that movement. If the opponent follows through as predicted, then that allows Paul to grab him and break the arm. (You might call that checkmate.) At each stage of the contest he anticipates about three moves ahead, considering alternatives and adjustments as the fight plays out: if this, then that; if that, then this.

"It's not just a brutal, violent sport. You have to think, and the people who think it through, relax, and maintain their composure do much, much better than the guys who go in there full force and just fight, fight, fight without thinking.

"You have a tremendous number of options on moves. Every move that you make, the other person has a world of responses that are possible. Based on how he reacts to your movement, you then have to counter his." You narrow your opponent's options as time goes on.

Yes, it is possible to have your arm broken or break someone else's, but Paul has been in one piece for a long time, which demonstrates, among other things, the protective power of contingency thinking.

Now, I have to admit that I was wrong about something when I heard Paul's story, because I made an automatic assumption that, just because he's a litigator, a passion for courtroom battles is a natural outcropping of his love for martial arts. It is not; the stronger attraction really is for the "chess of the fight."

"If I could do jujitsu all day long and not practice law, I would do it in a heartbeat," he says. Paul's excellent record as a student gave him lots of options in terms of acceptance into graduate schools. With no particular drive toward law, he entered law school and subsequently became a securities lawyer. A prestigious firm had a need, and he met it. His entrepreneurial spirit took hold very quickly, however, and he took off on his own.

When he says "I'm just as much a businessperson as I am a lawyer," he's lived that assertion. With one other lawyer, he formed a new firm that quickly grew to 35 attorneys with three offices. Paul served as managing partner, handling the range of decisions related to staffing and finances, as well as his litigation load. He merged that firm with the largest law firm in his practice area.

"I have no doubt that years and years of martial arts training contributed to my ability to achieve my business success. The mental discipline, the ability to think under pressure, to maintain a cool head have all served me well.

"When you're on the ground under a guy who's 250 pounds of pure muscle and could choke the life out of you, you have to think with a calm head. You think, I'm in a stressful situation. I've been here before. I can survive this. If I just adjust my leverage, I can flip him. I can start to breathe again.

"When you compare that to having 18 deadlines in one day and having a judge on the phone who's upset with you and a client who demands that you get to the phone right away and a secretary who's mad because another secretary offended her, the training comes into play." Paul takes a deep breath, sets priorities, links options to them, and moves with the anticipation of countermoves.

"The ability to think ahead, to anticipate moves, means the difference between winning and losing," he says. "You must have contingencies."

Know What Causes Bad Outcomes

There are five primary reasons for bad outcomes:

◆ Tunnel vision
◆ Ignoring instincts
◆ Poor judgment
◆ Overconfidence
◆ Random events

Contingency thinking can help you deal with them and in some cases even derail the movement toward disaster.

Tunnel Vision

Tunnel vision means obsessively focusing on a goal or single activity to the point where you or members of your team lose peripheral vision. That kind of behavior is often equated with a savage desire to win, but the downside is it's too easy to be blindsided by competitors, shifts in the customer needs, and a plethora of other conditions in a dynamic market. And then there are the weaknesses and glitches internal to the company that suddenly surface. The executive who goes into every project asking "What's our plan if this or that happens?" is not someone likely to suffer from the ill effects of tunnel vision.

Ignoring Instincts

Ignoring a gut feeling is not always a triumph of logic over that nebulous power called *intuition*, or *instinct*. You might be surprised to know how many times our mountaineer-executives did not describe events like avalanches as "accidents." Despite evidence to the contrary, they had a feeling that all was not well on the mountain that day. A reasonable explanation, for those who don't believe in a sixth sense, is that when you're good at something your radar for disaster is fine-tuned. It's the same in a business deal. Something about the project, the client, or the team dynamic just does not feel right. Pull back. Give yourself another day to evaluate the deal. Get the team together to review plans and proposals line by line. Combine analysis and gut feeling to create an effective decision-making process.

Aerobatic pilot and instructor Bob Stangarone, vice president of corporate communications for Cessna, offers this definition of instinct: "how you would naturally react to a stimulus based on all of your experiences." He believes you can get to a high level of performance only by engaging your instinct and that you will stop short in your ascent in business if you don't engage your instinct.

"You start out where your intellect is of greatest value, but as you build experience and experiences, you move more into relying on instinct. Things become more second nature.

"I'm a great believe in psycho-cybernetics [the system of success conditioning techniques pioneered by Dr. Maxwell Maltz]. I believe there are things we build into our brain that get stored there and processed and come out in ways we don't think about. I think that's the kind of thing that drives us to go from intellect to instinct."

Poor Judgment

No matter how smart or how capable you are, occasionally you will fall victim to a mistake in judgment that leaves you vulnerable. When you find yourself in the midst of a bad call, look for the underlying cause. Inadequate preparation? Underestimating the challenge? Spur-of-the-moment decision? How you regroup and move on depends on your knowledge of why your judgment was flawed in the first place.

Focus on matching your decision-making process with the real time you have in which to make the decision. If you have a situation in which a decision can be considered over time, then put yourself on a path of research, meetings to exchange ideas, and reflection so that your decision reflects the amount of time you had. Like Bob Stangarone in his role at Cessna, you often do not have that luxury. Bob might have minutes to prepare for an interview with a journalist about a crisis situation; he has to make a decision quickly about how he's going to handle it.

For him, the analogy in aerobatic flying is the need to make a lot of decisions in a matter of seconds. The lesson for anyone is "Don't put off a decision that is necessary to make now."

Know the difference between having that imperative and being in a situation where you do have the time. In the latter situations the "necessity" is that you take the time. For example, when you are preparing for a flight and your schedule is flexible, you can leisurely evaluate the weather conditions. You can go at the ideal time, not create an artificial pressure that will result in unnecessary demands or risks.

Many decisions in business are that way. But the ability to make a decision quickly is a great strength that should be cultivated and used when the requirement to act hits quickly.

For a pilot, training in a simulator helps to hone that skill. Flight simulators represent the real world and provide skill exercises that will help pilots fly in the real world. But since they aren't, in fact, the real world, the perceived risk goes way down. Crash a simulator; walk away. That's precisely why it's valuable to stretch the skill set. Pilots can do things in a simulator that they would not intentionally do in an airplane. It's not a substitute for flying, of course. At some point they still have to fly the airplane; otherwise they're just pilots in a really sophisticated video game.

Similarly, there is nothing like real life experience to ground you in how things really work in business, but that doesn't negate the value of going through exercises to sharpen your decision-making skills. Two business versions of simulator training are continuing education and crisis planning.

Bob has a very fresh take on crisis planning since he can anticipate that his industry will have ups and downs based on shifting economic conditions, fuel prices, the cost of raw materials, and a number of other variables that remain fluid.

In the 2002–2003 time frame, Cessna faced a downturn in which the company had to cut production and employees. In anticipation of a similar downtrend in 2008, the management team went back and looked at what happened the last time, at what drove the business down or up, and then used that as the basis for deciding what the options were likely to be in 2008. A major new factor came into the scenario they were building, however: the escalation in the role of international markets. In the five years between one economic downturn and the next, they had to look at a sizable portion of their orders in a different light. They could no longer count on international orders to help them get through the tight times.

Creating the scenario and targeting the options even slightly ahead of when sectors of the economy started to unravel at a rapid rate gave them a vision of how to land on a dirt strip or a cornfield rather than slam into the side of a mountain. It gave them time to consider how to manage things like voluntary layoff packages, which was one of the things they offered employees at production facilities where cuts later had to occur.

A crisis plan like this is just like the emergency checklists Bob relies on in flying. It is designed to set up a logical sequence for decision making when an event actually hits.

Overconfidence
Overconfidence is the fourth preventable cause on the list and, next to tunnel vision, probably the biggest source of trip-ups for success-driven people. Based on all of the interviews we did, it's safe to say this is less of a problem for people on top than it is for people on their way to the top. For that reason, you might call overconfidence an element of "sophomore syndrome," that state of having learned a lot and made enough progress that you sometimes think, What can go wrong that I can't handle? The reality is that a lot can go wrong, and you may not have the experience to cope with it. Keep in mind that you may be born with talent, but not with the knowledge of how to mitigate risk. That comes with experience.

Random Events
While you cannot stop a random event, you can be reasonably prepared for it. The people starting to prepare Q3 2001 reports the morning the planes struck the World Trade Center Towers could do very little to change the impact the attack would have on Q3, but they could certainly start immediately to influence how the attack would affect Q4 results. Determining

responses in advance to seemingly random events is a vital part of the role of communications professionals and loss prevention departments in most large organizations.

At Cessna, as well as the other aviation manufacturing companies that he's served in senior communications roles, Bob Stangarone developed contingency plans—sometimes called *crisis plans*—for airplane crashes, strikes, plant closings, factory shootings, and a host of other events. Some are truly random and occur with no warning, while for others a slim window of warning is all he got.

In any extreme sports situation, these events will occur in the form of a rogue wave, an avalanche, or an explosion spooking your horse. You have to know what they might be and prepare to respond. On both a personal and a team level, you have the same requirement in business. Pinpoint what those "random" events might be and get ready for them.

Think Your Way Through Potential Disasters

Surfers and Surf Diva founders Izzy and Coco Tihanyi have a contingency plan mind-set. In fact, Coco states one of her business mottos as "If you have a really good Plan B, then Plan A usually works out."

The roots of the mind-set probably come from the fact that the key success factor in surfing, according to Izzy and Coco, is safety. And the main part of safety is not to panic; have a plan to get you out of the jam. Izzy says, "If you panic as you're being swept toward rocks, you'll probably drown. So don't fight the current; go with the flow. If you're being caught in a riptide, don't swim against the tide. Swim perpendicular to it, parallel to the beach, and then find your escape route and catch a wave in where the waves are breaking. Don't try to catch a wave when there aren't any."

In their business, too, they look at safety as number one. In that context they define it as being proactive about educating yourself and taking risks knowing that you have a safety valve in place.

An example is that, in October 2008, when people around the world sank into mental depression about the state of the economy, Izzy and Coco ordered a new set of boards for the 2009 season. They needed them for the school, but they also had a safety valve in case all of the expected students never showed up. Coco got the boards at a reduced rate because she was buying them off season. She also bought a board design that is perfect for the school but also has retail value. She did not buy those quirky-looking boards you see hotels making available to their guests that a real surfer would never be seen on.

Coco says, "We're always thinking the glass is half full and half empty at the same time." If a risk does pay off, then great, and if it doesn't, they have a backup plan because they've looked at the possibility of the negative outcome.

CHAPTER 23

Take the Extra Step:

Push to the Edge

MARATHONER QUANG X. Pham, founder and CEO of Lathian Health, didn't begin running seriously until he was in his early forties. Like other commitments he had made in his life, such as serving in war as a Marine Corps helicopter pilot, he prepared aggressively so he could succeed. In getting ready to run long distances, he not only ran but also learned from the best about how to run better. He watched videos on YouTube, visited websites on running, and researched what top runners had to say about training.

It's clear the same degree of commitment goes into his fitness as a business leader. Quang trains hard—harder than others—in pursuit of excellence. His lesson: "Take the extra step. Push to the edge."

"So when I think about marathons, having started a company, raised venture capital, written a book—they are all very similar. You can't write a book in two weeks, just like you can't prepare for a marathon in two weeks. It's a process. It takes discipline, mental and physical endurance." And to do it well, the "push" needs to be a consistent part of the process. Taking the extra step must become habitual.

Find Out What You, Others, and Your Organization Are Truly Capable Of

Push on an individual level to boost personal performance. Push circumstances to achieve a level of engagement with your team that you otherwise wouldn't get. You want to set things up so that people who respond to you in your organization feel momentum to exceed their perceived limits.

The environment you create should allow you and the members of your team to push the limits. Most of us perform at a level less than we're capable of reaching, but that level will likely go up when we surround ourselves with people who are pushing toward higher standards.

Use goals and meaningful metrics of success to help stir up this energy. Some people will find audacious goals threatening; others will find them exciting. Assess the personalities of people on your team so that you inspire them with a goal that makes them (and you) stretch, but not something so outrageous that they find it either laughable or paralyzing. Set up a goal that makes people say, "Man, I don't want to be on the sidelines when that happens!" Intoxicate them with possibilities.

Use failures to your advantage in developing a strategy to achieve the goal. If people on the team resist an audacious goal because "we tried something like this before and it didn't work," take inventory of the lessons learned in that previous attempt. Take advantage of the wisdom and insights garnered from the failed attempt so that you don't make any of the same mistakes. You can legitimately argue that you are better prepared to succeed than you were before you failed.

Computer industry rebel Apple began innovating in the area of handheld devices in the early 1990s and produced a near total failure with the Newton MessagePad. Nevertheless, the product led to the birth of a new category of appliances and, eventually, the creation of a worldwide sensation: iPhone. The folks at Apple must have learned something from the earlier struggle.

If you expect every innovation to be successful, you'll never innovate.

Use Metrics to Keep the Momentum Going

Olympic bobsledder Gord Woolley connects strongly with performance measurements. As a competitor in bobsledding, he felt that the multiple metrics involved with evaluating his physical condition, such as weight, body composition, and strength, coupled with the absolute of performance—time of the run—gave him definite signals about how to improve. So he has always incorporated metrics into his performance evaluation. His business involves a huge number of measurable steps, including the creation, assembly, delivery, and placement of printed materials, allowing his appreciation of the "numbers of success" to serve him well. It also gives his employees a clear indication of how they can evaluate their performance at any given time.

Quang Pham says the same thing about the satisfaction he gets from running marathons: you always know your times, so you always know how well you did. Same in business: you know what the bottom line is. Problem is, you always know your times, so you know when you sink to a low point too.

And this, Quang says, is when you really push in both running and business: "Your endurance in business is really tested when times get tough, just

Troy Widgery, founder and president of Go Fast Sports and Beverage Company, landing after a base jump off the 1,053-foot-high Royal Gorge bridge in Colorado

as your endurance in running is tested when you are exhausted." His prime example: he burned through nearly all of the $5 million start-up capital he won in the national contest that helped him launch MyDrugRep.com. Quang had a staff of 25 and only two weeks' payroll remaining. This was the end of 2000 and the disheartening beginning of the dot-com bust. He had built a company almost overnight and suddenly found himself nearly out of money.

Quang found some new metrics to apply.

"Some people say when you're going through a rough time like this, take a step back, take a deep breath, and analyze everything. I go with the Colin Powell approach—you got 40 percent, start taking action, adjust it at 70 percent, you'll never have 100 percent of the answers, but you just have to take action. Reminds me of one of the Marine mottoes: 'Dammit, Lieutenant. Do something!' In other words, don't just sit there and get your platoon killed while you're still thinking about what to do."

And so Quang raised more money and took the company to a new level. His lesson: "There are milestones to check yourself out for mental endurance just as you can check yourself out for physical endurance. You can build up your mental endurance."

When Maryann was training for her second Eco-Challenge Endurance Race, one of her team captains was a former Navy SEAL. He tapped into the mentality that metrics can give a sense of progress by occasionally calling out, "Yell out when we've gone another three klicks!" It became a game, since he had the tracking information to indicate exactly when they had gone three klicks, or three kilometers, but it was a game that reduced the boredom to some extent. Two teammates gave the answer by gut; they decided to just talk on the trail and give an estimate based on feeling. Another two teammates counted paces. Their "yells" were always more accurate. The value of that was, in the race, when there were no electronic gadgets and no one had the energy to converse on the trail, it was important for practical and emotional reasons to be able to answer the questions, "How much farther?" and "How far have we come?"

As Quang suggests, you need to pay attention to the milestones so that you have a basis for self-evaluation and for setting expectations for the next stage of performance.

Engage Your Imagination

Imagination is a core element of performance improvement.

I grew up with Americans in business, politics, academia, and every other walk of life saying, "You know, if we can put a man on the moon, we can (fill in the blank)." There is clearly no relationship between the technology to put a man on the moon and closing an enormous real estate deal, but that's not the point. The man on the moon represents the ability to dream big and then realize the dream through concerted action.

Troy Widgery, skydiver, BASE (building, antenna, span, earth) jumper, and founder and president of Go Fast Sports and Beverage Company, decided to build a jet pack—like what you'd find in a James Bond movie. Troy was not going to build just any jet pack, but something that ran on relatively affordable fuel and had the potential of becoming a vehicle afford-able to entities other than the U.S. Defense Department. After two years of development he succeeded. In the summer of 2008, Troy's jet pack made its debut. His current model is capable of providing 33 seconds of continuous flight, and his forthcoming high-end model will provide nine minutes of continuous flight, which is a lot more consumer friendly than the 23-second flights that the original Bell Aerosystems jet pack provided.

But it's not just a jet pack to the team at Go Fast. When Troy decided to expand the company's product line with energy gum, there were all kinds of reasons why it didn't look like that idea would take shape. Troy turned the naysayers around with "Hey, we built a jet pack. We can find a way." It's the tangible, homegrown version of putting a man on the moon.

CHAPTER 24

Try Groping
in the Dark:

Be Fluid

CHERYL TRAVERSE, PRESIDENT and CEO of Xceedium, started scuba diving at the age of 12 just because she knew somebody who had the gear. She grew up in Pennsylvania, and in the summertime, her family lived at a lake. Figuring she'd already explored the top five feet of the lake, Cheryl saw no reason not to borrow the neighbor's scuba equipment and make some dives. One of the older kids at the lake yelled at her: "You're gonna kill yourself if you keep doing that! Let me teach you."

She dove day after day, exploring as much of the 40-foot depths as she could. There was only one real impediment to her adventure: she couldn't see anything down there. Now, in her business, when the path ahead seems murky, she says, "This is like scuba diving in a freshwater lake."

Cheryl would grope along the bottom in the darkness, driven by sheer curiosity. One day it paid off: "I found a pioneer canoe." She alerted other kids at the lake, who then worked together with her for an entire weekend to rescue the canoe, made from a hollowed-out tree, which had been submerged for about 150 years. It now sits in the Everhart Museum in Scranton, Pennsylvania.

It was the newness and the strangeness of the environment that drew her, and she says it was nothing more complicated than that. It is the same reason she thrives on leading start-up companies: "I don't like to retrace my steps. I like to move forward and find new adventurous things to do."

Along with that curiosity goes an amazing ability to see opportunities where others might not. You don't plan to find a canoe at the bottom of the lake, but it's certainly possible.

She emphasizes that this cannot be done without confidence and a good deal of adaptability. Both come into play in determining "That's not the right way; let's do it differently." Staying the course may seem like the safe thing to do, but if you're in a start-up company, many times that approach will kill you.

Recognize That Adapting Is Gaining Strength, Not Compromising It

When the nature of her chief executive job changed as the company grew and she no longer focused almost solely on market shifts and product development, cyclist Deidre Paknad faced the growing requirement to manage people at PSS Systems. It's not something she wanted to do. At first she resented the need to put her personal resources into that, but then she thought about the lesson of her cycling—that it's just another part of the same ride. She also thought that, just because she'd been on that ride before didn't mean she didn't have a huge need to get to the top. She still had the drive to get to the place with the great view: "One day you tackle a hill and feel so strong doing it, and the next day or week you can tackle the same hill and feel miserable." She adapted, as a cyclist and a CEO.

She sees that adapting like this will help her take the company to SAP size. Why not? "They started with the same-color whiteboard we did."

Be Sensitive to Market Signals

Cheryl Traverse is now heading up her sixth successful start-up as president of Xceedium. She sees her awareness of market signals and agile, organized response to their changes as being a big part of her job—it's called moving the buoys: "I drive the company. I look at it as a sailing race. I come in and develop a plan. I put all the buoys in the water for the sailing race. It's my job to keep track of the winds and determine if the buoys are in the right or wrong place and then move them."

Sometimes she has found that she moves the buoys too soon when it's clear that the competitive environment or market conditions have shifted, for example. But in most cases she believes in a bias for action. The ramifications of moving the buoys too soon pale in comparison to not moving them soon enough.

In sailing, as in climbing and many other outdoor sports, you are always managing your response to time and weather. Think of time and weather as the

Cheryl Traverse, president/CEO of Xceedium, sailing on the notoriously challenging San Francisco Bay
Shannon McIntyre, 2007

equivalent to your market signals, the largely uncontrollable (at least by a single individual) competitive and market forces that profoundly affect your business. They are changing all the time, and your adeptness in recognizing even small changes will determine whether you look like a strategic and tactical genius or an average or disappointing performer.

Cheryl was sailing in the Greek Islands and came into port with many other boats during a storm that drove the winds up to 65 knots. She anchored but noticed that the people upwind had not anchored properly for the conditions. She knew that, as the storm came in, those boats would crash into her boat, as well as others. She could leave the port in the wild winds or remain and face almost certain disaster. To complicate matters, the captain of the nearby boat was inebriated; his inability to act meant that he would push all of the boats downwind of him if his boat became another weapon of the wind. So Cheryl and her fellow sailors in the area climbed on board and secured it.

The next day she was back in the open ocean with eight-foot swells and 40-knot winds—sounds a lot like start-up conditions for a business. Cheryl put a storm jib out on the bow, significantly reducing sail area so as not to capsize the boat, and hung an anchor off the stern to minimize pivoting of the boat as it was hit by swells and waves. Her unusual and creative actions balanced the boat, and they made headway.

This kind of situation puts you at a fork in the decision-making road: take a course of action as close as possible to your original plan and you may achieve 80 percent of your goal instead of 100 percent, or change course based on the new conditions with the possibility of getting exactly what you want.

A classic business example is pursuing a new distribution channel, and this is not only classic but also a real issue facing Cheryl's company. Currently she has a plan to develop a distributor network that her company did not have before, as they rely on direct sales. This is a standard part of the maturation process for a company, initially focusing on direct sales because it provides control. In addition, dealers are not likely to be responsive to a company with little or no market share. Her company has now reached that point where it has the market share to interest dealers. With the position and credibility to develop new distribution channels, Cheryl has to move the buoys. There is a shifting sea of competitors out there vying for the same channels, and the marketing strategy to reach them has to consider myriad variables that it previously did not. Among them is how the competitors might try to sweeten existing deals to block her company's entry.

There may be a science to when you change course in a boat race, but when you change course in business it is more art than science. Cheryl notes that she thrives on information and relies heavily on metrics, yet 40 percent of what influences her business decisions is instinct. The science is the information from her engineering, marketing, and other pros, as well as other data sources. The instinct is the combination of experience, innate talent, and sensitivities to the shifting winds that make her judgment uniquely valuable.

Per Welinder's combination of art and science in reading market signals is fundamental to his success from the moment he envisions a new product line. After founding eight companies aimed at a male youth market, he knows that his consumers can change tastes and purchasing patterns as often as they change underwear.

The first part of Per's strategy is scientific, or analytical: "When you create an idea, have a consumer in mind. Who is the person? What does he associate with? Whom does he associate with? What music does he listen to? Does he have siblings that he likes or doesn't like? What activities does he have?" Starting with those levels of connection gives Per a strong sense of what resonates with that individual consumer who represents his target. His core audience is the 16-year-old looking for his own identity. A lot of them are followers, whose greatest desire is to be part of a tribe. They look to the magnet so they can firmly establish themselves as having the right clothes and listening to the right music. Feeding into the tribal phenomenon, and even engendering changes in it, gives companies like Per's an impressive chunk of success acreage—until the tribe morphs again.

The second step is a mechanism for influencing the market signals. He identifies the "magnets," that is, the style and opinion influencers. If you go to any school or work environment, there will always be people who are perceived as leaders. Particularly when marketing to teenagers, an executive has to know who those leaders are to get a specific sense of whose early adoption of a product will influence sales immediately. Per builds brands for young adults, so identifying those people is a core business objective. Those targets change yearly if not more often. Someone who wore the brand when he was 16 and is now 20 may be so out of touch with what 16-year-olds wear that his endorsement is useless—or worse. In Per's business, these people are a moving target.

When young people love a brand, it can translate into a passionate brand loyalty, so the market signal stays strong and predictable for a while. Apple saw this with iPod, to the extent that people without earbuds became cultural foreigners to the devotees. Similarly, Per seeks to identify the leaders, turn them into early adopters, engage their passion about the brand, and then turn them loose into their market and let their appearance have an evangelical effect.

And then, as the composition of the market changes—that is, ages—he goes through the whole process again.

CHAPTER 25

"Dude, What's Up with the Bull Riding?"

Focus Outward

AS THE CHIEF executive of Versus television, Gavin Harvey invests personally in the customer experience. That is, he engages in the sports he's covering on his network; if he doesn't participate in them, he watches them. So, when he negotiates contracts with people like Professional Bull Riders president Ty Murray, he does so as an authentic participant.

He believes so strongly in this approach to understanding his customers, in fact, that his colleagues in other industries sometimes find it a little weird:

"When I'm cycling with a bunch of executives and they say, 'Dude, what's up with the bull riding?' I need to be able to say, 'Have you ever been to a bull-riding event? Do you know how incredibly tough bull riders are? How much training they go through? How much pain they play with? These guys are studs. They're my heroes.'"

Gavin can say that honestly because he's been there. He knows the sports and who is involved in them. None of this was accidental. He guided himself into jobs where he could really invest his interest and have the passion for the content, including E! Networks, where he spearheaded sophisticated

Dennis Sponer, founder, president, and CEO of ScripNet, competing in the Las Vegas Half Marathon

rebranding initatives for both E! Entertainment Television and the Style Network. Without hesitation, he can answer the question of why his audience is so passionate about the programming.

"The network is like religion to some people. I want to understand that from their angle. At Versus, we worship the challenge. The man *versus* man, team *versus* team, country *versus* country—the drama of competition whether it's in a stadium or a wilderness. That's how we can form a cohesive brand promise."

ScripNet's founder and CEO, Dennis Sponer, has his own take on understanding things from the customer's perspective. Sometimes he will go to visit a client and do a run in the area before the meeting to get familiar with the client's office neighborhood. It creates a dimension of connection with the client that just showing up at the door would never do. By the time they sit down to talk, he knows what kind of traffic his client has to deal with in getting to work and how far he has to go to get a great cup of coffee. And when he's on the phone with him later, he can connect with the client's references to local weather and street noise.

Don't Try to Make Your Life Easier at the Expense of Your Customers' and Clients' Needs, or the Company Will Flounder

Ever have an experience with an airline or bank, in a grocery store, or with a credit card company that makes you wonder, Whom is that policy intended to serve? A lot of actions by companies supposedly in the business of serving the public seem more designed for their convenience than for the customers'. Worse yet, a lot of actions seem to be taken at the expense of their clients or customers.

Recently I was at a restaurant in a resort town during the off-season. To restaurateurs, that means "there were no customers." The hostess seated my friend and me at a lovely table for two. Shortly afterward, she seated a party of five at the table next to us. This was not a malicious act intended to destroy any chance of having a quiet conversation. She acted out of convenience to the one server working that night. Customer service took a backseat to a policy of seating according to a chart that reflected who was on duty.

This is not just a problem exhibited on a consumer-by-consumer basis, either. Lots of large companies have thrown their suppliers under the bus. For example, GM did such a good job of reducing the prices it was willing to pay its suppliers that it drove a number of them out of business. Pinhead thinking destroyed an industry and then led to pinhead questions like "Gosh, where did all the suppliers go?" Cut your vendors' margins so they can't even keep a workforce, much less reinvest in innovation, and you kill the vendors and perhaps even an industry.

A prime example of a company whose executive leadership does not seem to look outward is United Airlines. They apparently have no problem taking actions that make their lives easier at the expense of their customers. United Airlines employees will force you to stand in line to use a kiosk even when you don't want to or know your transaction cannot be executed at that particular kiosk. I know this personally because I happened to be a "misidentified person," that is, inadvertently placed on the airline watch list, for a while and couldn't use kiosks to check in. Repeatedly I would find a real person, explain that I couldn't use the kiosk, be told that I had to try to use the kiosk first, and then get assistance only after it was clear that I couldn't check in using the kiosk.

Many policies I've observed seem to serve the company, not its customer base. Any company that is willing to pursue operational efficiencies at the expense of the customer experience is moving in the wrong direction, toward a state of decline. There is an air of desperation in such moves.

Take a Customer-Centric Approach to Build Business

Three of the athlete-executives in this book were so committed to putting their customers' needs ahead of their own that they rebelled against the way their industries charged customers. Their innovative minds and contrarian approach to industry practices caused them to launch operations that eliminated pricing systems designed to benefit company over client.

In 1991, long before the concept gained any popularity, Bob Travers, vice president of wealth management, Citi Smith Barney, decided to go to a fee-based system of serving clients. He found that the standard practice of churning assets, which meant generating income on the volume of transactions, created an inherently adversarial relationship between a broker and his clients. He took the approach of a financial planner to money management, rather than that of a stock jockey. In this model, he says, "The person who handles managed money actually makes less money, but it's in the best interests of everyone going forward. I had to suck it up for the first seven years, but in that time, my book [of business] got bigger and bigger." It led to his vice presidency and personal management of $100 million.

In 1993, Stacie Blair also set herself up as a billing pioneer in the executive search firm industry. In forming the Pacific Firm, Stacie bucked traditional models like charging a percentage of the compensation paid to the new recruit and simply charged on a per-hour basis. Clients felt relieved at having this kind of structure, and their loyalty and references led to a ranking in the top five recruiting firms in the San Francisco Bay area.

In 1995, Julie Pearl broke with a long-standing legal practice in setting up the policies for Pearl Law Group: she decided not to bill by the hour. This was about a year before former associate attorney general Webster Hubbell, in prison for tax evasion at the time, admitted something many people had long suspected about lawyers. In a conversation being recorded, his wife asked him if he had made up billed time for a client, since he had been accused of stealing $482,000 this way. He said yes and then asserted that every lawyer in the country does it.

"Most people don't recognize us as a typical law firm," she says. "What we do is a service business." Pearl Law Group behaves like a service business in every way. The firm's lawyers don't go to court. And they charge a flat fee for services. The unconventional approach certainly hasn't hurt, since her firm has made "Fastest Growing" lists and was named the number-one woman-owned law firm in the San Francisco Bay area.

Izzy and Coco Tihanyi also epitomize this customer-centric approach in the way they have built Surf Diva, their very successful surf school. It reflects what Izzy tried to bring to young women when she first started teaching at the University of California at San Diego.

Izzy worked her way through college there by giving surf lessons through the physical education department. The women gravitated to her classes rather than those taught by men because they felt more encouraged and less intimidated than with the male instructors. The "hot surfer guys" teaching the classes were not really there to teach; they weren't patient. Izzy, on the other hand, really wanted the female students to succeed, so she developed a teaching method that helped them make strong, steady progress. It's an adventure-based, nonjudgmental method that she refined over the years with other female surfing instructors, and it is the core program for Surf Diva, the world's leading surf school for women.

Over the years, the reputation of Surf Diva grew both because of the effective teaching method and because of an approach that made things fun—the twin sisters agree that the best surfer in the water is the one having the most fun. In 2003, they expanded by launching a program in Costa Rica, and it has grown remarkably every year since. Izzy and Coco took a look at the different elements that have made a difference and concluded that it completely reflected their philosophy, which Coco explains as follows: "We run our program as if it were our best friend going to Costa Rica. That's how we treat every student."

Time after time, the people we interviewed pinpointed attention to customers' and clients' convenience, as well as basic needs, as a key to success. I would describe what they talked about as a kind of active listening; that is, you not only hear the words that people speak to you but also pay attention to what isn't said that can suggest a deeper need or a deeper meaning.

The customer-centric approach to building business also plays into a type of thinking that John Wilson calls "boxing the risk."

Before John Wilson started J.C. Wilson Associates, he worked with Citibank in Asia and had prime responsibility for making loan recommendations. Clients were multinationals and Asian companies, and John had to have an eye for the trouble spots, as well as positive trends. "Boxing the risk" involved making sure that companies asking for Citibank's money knew where their cash flow was going to come from. That is, did they have a keen focus on both the needs of their prospective customers and where to find them? "If you're about to lend a company $10 or $20 million, you have to run the numbers, of course, but you also have to have a sense of where that industry is going, where that company is going, who their customers are. One risk that I was always on the lookout for was the borrower company being too dependent on one customer."

Ask Yourself, "Who Are We Trying to Please with This Change or Initiative?"

Consciously ask the question: is what we're doing for our benefit or for the benefit of our customers, clients, and suppliers? This exercise is not meant to suggest that "for our benefit" is a bad answer and that you should not take the action. Doing something to benefit yourself and not your customers is not inherently bad. The fact that you had the presence of mind to ask the question and honestly face the answer will help you put the decision into perspective.

You do not want to take that course of action consistently, though.

A sign that a company is in decline is that it repeatedly enforces decisions that serve the company more than its customers. From top to bottom, employees have to do this whether it's because they think they can get away with it or because serving themselves is their primary focus. They lack the critical awareness of how destructive that approach is over time.

The annals of climbing are replete with stories of falls with people roped together, dependent on each other's performance, but one person errs in judgment or loses his footing and sends himself and others plummeting. After it happens, and everyone lives, you may revisit your choices of acceptable climbing partners.

Know That Companies Guided by Their Customers' and Clients' Needs Raise the Bar

Contrast the behavior of some companies that reflects a lack of accountability and good judgment with the call I once got from Seth Schofield, former CEO of US Airways, after I registered a complaint about giving more desirable exit row seats to nonrevenue employee passengers. He actually called me at my office to tell me he had read my letter, felt the point I made was valid and the current policy lacked good sense, and put new orders in place immediately to change it. Similarly, Richard Branson met a challenge head on when a condom produced by one of his companies failed to perform as advertised. After conveying his apologies to the customer, he consented to becoming godfather to the child when it was born later that year.

These actions are not part of a guaranteed success formula, but they remove one more excuse for failure. They raise the bar in an environment in which consumers sometimes think companies are ventures of the Evil Empire. They humanize the experience of doing business.

I have worked with several companies guided by a CEO who periodically goes on sales calls. At the very least, a vice president or director of sales would want to go on calls occasionally to get direct feedback from customers and help reps improve their sales skills. This is not just a data-gathering exercise, but one that engages intuition and allows the person to observe customers' environments and ascertain whether personalities are well matched to make deals.

The FootJoy organization, a leading manufacturer of golf shoes, gloves, and clothing, took this model and improved on it. They have a handful of salespeople who are particularly experienced in relating to customers. The company brings them and their unique information back to the factory a couple of times a year. These professionals funnel customer feedback to the product development team. Because FootJoy executives don't want this added responsibility to penalize these salespeople, they put them on a different compensation program as long as they remain in that role.

Some companies, like Toro, establish this relationship with customers directly. People who buy a lot of snowblowers and lawn mowers for government agencies and companies get invited to spend a week at the factory and contribute their thoughts on product improvements.

You can do focus groups, polls, and surveys with potential customers all you want, but getting input from people who have had the experience of using your product or service does more to establish your organization as one that might actually care about serving its customers and clients. You learn valuable information while you strengthen a relationship.

CHAPTER 26

A Great Ride Isn't Going to Be an Easy Ride:

You Have to Find a Way

"Getting to the top is certainly not the goal. Doing it in the purest and most rewarding personal style is of greater importance. With enough equipment, you can get up any wall, but to do it free-climbing requires the most elegant methods. It requires the most training and greatest personal commitment, and it is the most rewarding for me. To struggle up a rock wall by pulling on this and hammering on that gets you to the top. But you can do it like a dance. That's the reward. I look at my business the same way.

"To attack a mountain with armies of people and porters and Sherpas carrying loads—there is no personal satisfaction in that. Virtually anything can be conquered that way, with enough time and enough equipment and enough people.

"To go into the mountains lightweight, with well-trained, well-equipped climbers with their experience and their abilities and to try a long technical route, or maybe an exploratory route, is an extraordinary adventure. Your chances of failure are greater,

*but so what? It's the journey. And the feeling that you're there because you're really
good at what you do."*

> —Mark Richey, president, Mark Richey Woodworking, a $20 million
> Massachusetts-based firm that employs 100 people and has won multiple
> awards related to architectural excellence

CYCLIST DEIDRE PAKNAD has a simple bit of advice that supports
Mark's insights and zeroes in on something you need to know to keep pushing toward success no matter what. She draws from the sweet pain of her
pushes up the hills in the San Francisco Bay area: "You have to have a tolerance for discomfort. A great ride isn't going to be an easy ride." When you
combine that tolerance—a mature patience coupled with persistence that
you build up over time and experience—with passion for what you do, you
will find a way. And when you're done, the view is spectacular.

Make It Work with What You Have—
Resources Are Always Limited

One of the most common complaints you will hear in business is "We could
have done it if we'd only had more cash, capital, people, time. . . ." The athletes who participate in activities that remove them from sources of supplies
and additional support all expressed something along the lines of "You have
what you have, so make it work." Swing back to the beginning of the book,
where I talked about the victim mentality. This is part of it. So the complementary lessons here are (1) don't make excuses for what you don't have and
(2) find a way to succeed with what you do have.

The experience of a pilot is the regular exercise of creating a successful
outcome with finite resources. You can equip a plane with the best avionics,
but there comes a point when, even with "unlimited" resources, fancier avionics would not improve the situation all that much because the plane itself
has certain limitations.

As pilot and CAE executive Jeff Roberts says, "In flying, you have what
you have. You have to take what you have and use it to create a successful

end. Some days, the weather is great, the plane works well, and you are at the top of your game. Other days, there are events that cause your environment to change, but you have to find a way to create the same kind of successful end."

In business, as in flying, the successful decision maker learns from the process of attempting to succeed with limited resources. You realize you have to learn more about the weather or about the chain of events that caused you to end up in the tough situation you were in. You do a lot of assessment, review, and analysis in flying to answer the question "How did I end up here?" There is always a chain of events that leads you to either the success

Mark Richey makes his way along the spectacular East Ridge of Shivling during an alpine ascent of the Himalayan peak in India. John Bouchard, 1996

you hoped for and predicted or the unpleasant outcome that you never want to replicate again. Take time to analyze that chain of events in business.

The hard part is realizing there is a chain of events and tracking it accurately so you can learn from it.

Approach the Challenge from a Different Angle

Don Bell, who has about 90 starts in pro racing in the American Le Mans series to his credit, now sponsors a team in the series through his multi-billion-dollar company, Bell Microproducts. He makes a big point of saying that the driver may be the one steering the car and taking the risks on the track, but the ideas about how to win can also come from the crew, the owner, and the sponsors. And sometimes the same idea that didn't work one day will work another day—it just depends on the setup.

He cites races that were "won in the pits"; that is, the creative thinking of a clever team manager named Tony Dowe directly impacted the outcome of the race. Of particular note is a race in Florida that was close but where the lead seemed out of reach.

The cars were running nose to tail in a street race in St. Petersburg, and Don's Bell Ferrari was in third place. It was toward the end of the race and just about time for everyone to come in for tires and fuel. Tony lined everyone up in the pit, hands on tires, and called the driver in. Everyone else saw that and decided to time their fueling and tire changes to coincide. All the cars came flying into the pits. The Bell crew then fueled their car and sent it off with the old tires. "We got out before everyone else and went on to win the race," Don says.

The feint had some big risks associated with it, the most pronounced of which was that the tires wouldn't make it through to the end. What made it an intelligent risk was a reliable and predictable car and a team that could quickly weigh the risk *versus* the benefit.

Victories claimed by ideas and skills in the pit, in the car, and in the boardroom put the Bell car on top in 2008. By virtue of the win in Monterey at the season finale on October 18, the No. 71 Tafel/Bell Micro Racing Ferrari F430 GTC won more GT2 victories in 2008 than any other entry.

Stay Curious

In the course of the interviews, I learned that every athlete-executive in the book has the curiosity gene. It's the desire to try something new, to look around the corner and see something surprising. In Mark Richey's world of architectural woodworking, he sees building things they have never built before as an adventure: "If I had to build the same thing over and over again, I'd become terribly bored. Building new things fascinates me. With my climbing, it's about traveling to places I've never been before, trying some climb I've never tried before. The adventure is about the unknown. Going into places I'm a little uncomfortable about and seeing where we end up." For all of them, satisfying that curiosity involves taking risks with calculation.

Without human spirit, landing a 900 on a skateboard and summiting K2 are just terms to describe robotic feats. Many of the athlete-executives talked about their intangible skills as the real reason they can push the limits so far in both sport and business—and these skills are what you've seen described here as "success lessons from the edge." Intelligent risk taking sharpens their senses, expands their minds, and puts them on a fast track to self-discovery. Just when you thought they couldn't do anything more impressive, they do.

I believe we spend our lives seeking a transcendent experience. From people like the athlete-executives we featured in this book, we will continue to gain insights that can provide us with those experiences.

CONCLUSION

YOU NOW HAVE the benefit of the success lessons of adventurous men and women who applied them to both their careers and their sports. You probably picked up this book because you can connect with those lessons—maybe you already rely on some of them, or maybe you deeply admire people who do. That connection will help you take the step that can change your life, not just your career: act on these lessons every day.

Since you know how these athlete-executives got to where they are through their stories, you know they didn't have one or two days a week in which they honored their passion. They did it consistently. Waves of integrity didn't wash over them one day, and then the next day they cheated someone on a deal. No. They regularly relied on the principles of success presented in these pages.

They might have had off days, of course, and so will you. That's where your connection to the lessons comes in. If you were inspired by someone in your life to take a closer look at how adventurous successful people climbed to the summits of their careers, let that person know. We need to be grateful for the people in our own backyards who serve as role models. CEOs and senior executives have not cornered the market on lessons for success. The woman who has a pie shop down the street may be a finer example of someone who honors passion, practices resilience, and knows her limitations than anyone else you will ever meet. Open your eyes to the mentors and coaches around you.

Or maybe you have seen some of the people in this book on television or read an article about them, and that's what drew you to know more about them. Don't be shy about putting your favorite quote from that person on your wall as a reminder of whom you want to "grow up" to be and where you want to go with your career. You could be 22 right now, or you could be 52. Regardless of how old you are, you most likely have a lot of time left to make big, positive changes, but you need to act with urgency in conjunction with your newfound persistence.

Make the information in this book practical in your life. This is not a book to read and then discuss at a quilting club. Use the success factors to build your business. Use them to get yourself to the level where high performers operate. Use them to inspire your unique take on what traits lead to success.

Climb your mountain. Sail across your sea. Run your race. Ride your bull. Make a difference. Aspire to be great—in business and sport. The decision is yours.

APPENDIX A

Profiles of the Featured Athlete-Executives

Mike Angiulo

Leading a billion-dollar business as Microsoft Corporation's general manager of Microsoft Office Project Business Unit sounds scary, but what is scary for most is business as usual for Mike, an aerobatic pilot and paragliding pioneer. Mike has twelve hundred hours of multiengine time, has owned five airplanes including a Pit Special, and has flown from Long Island to Seattle in an open-cockpit biplane. Most active in aerobatic competitions in 2003, that year he won or placed in several regional competitions in a row and then won the Northwest Regional Champion Award. He went from there to Pylon Racing School at the Reno Air Races, where he participated in the pilot qualification school, which involved close-quarters aerobatics, flying below a hundred feet, and a whole series of other maneuvers to qualify him for wingtip-to-wingtip racing.

Shellye Archambeau

Shellye had a job before the school day ever began: clean the local stables as a trade for boarding fees for her horse, Scarborough, who became her partner in dressage. To her the appeal of the sport was what some might see as the extreme nature of it: a high degree of precision in guiding the horse through gymnastic maneuvers with minimal input from the rider. Shellye is chief executive officer of MetricStream, Inc. As a dressage competitor, she won several regional competitions on the East Coast. As a corporate executive, she has received many honors, including a Trailblazer Award at the Sixth Annual FWE Celebration of Leadership Achievement. She is a member of the Information Technology Senior Management Forum, the Forum of Women Entrepreneurs, and the Women's Council to the Board of Trustees for the University of Pennsylvania. She is also director of Silicon Valley Leadership Group, a nonprofit organization that addresses major public policy issues affecting the economic health and quality of life in Silicon Valley.

William F. Baker

Bill has earned awards and honors that stretch as far as both—the North and South Poles, where he has visited in the 1970s and 1980s. One of the very few people to take expeditions to the poles in that period, he was also a pioneer in public broadcasting and is now president emeritus of Educational Broadcasting Corporation in New York. Bill

227

holds a doctorate in industrial psychology in addition to honorary degrees from Rutgers University, Manhattan College, Fordham University, and many other institutions of higher learning. He is also a fellow of the Explorers Club—recognized by this prestigious professional society as having made documented contributions to exploration or scientific knowledge. He also produced the Emmy-winning documentary *The Face: Jesus in Art*. His current passion is lighthouse keeping for weeks at a time in remote locations, an extreme activity he can do with his wife.

David Becker

President and cofounder of PhilippeBecker, a San Francisco branding and packaging agency, David is also a skydiver, skydiving instructor, and coach. His team (Focus4) won silver medals at U.S. Nationals Skydiving competitions in 1998 and 2000. Under David's leadership, PhilippeBecker has increased revenue 1,700 percent from 2002 to 2007, grown to a team of 24 employees, won the prestigious HOW and Communication Arts awards, and been named by *Inc.* magazine to its 2007 list of America's 5,000 fastest-growing private companies. Sales for new brands that PhilippeBecker has created exceed $1 billion.

W. Donald (Don) Bell

Having about 90 starts in pro racing in the American Le Mans series to his credit was not enough, so Don took a "family trip" with his wife to the North Pole with David Hempleman-Adams, the first man in history to reach the geographic and magnetic North and South Poles as well as climb the highest peaks in all seven continents. Don is the founder, president, CEO, and chairman of the board of Bell Microproducts, one of the world's largest value-added distributors of storage and computing technology. Well respected among his peers, Don has gained a reputation for being an innovative strategist and a leader in creative high-tech marketing and management. Since its founding in 1988, Bell Microproducts has rocketed to a spot among the top five companies worldwide in its industry. Bell Microproducts sales exceed $4 billion.

Kirby Best

The former CEO of Ingram Lightning Source, the subsidiary of Ingram Industries Inc. that provides print-on-demand services, was on the Canadian ski and bobsled teams and with the latter took fourth place in 1983 World Cup. All together, he had competed internationally in 8 different sports: gymnastics, rugby, rowing, downhill racing, freestyle skiing, speed skiing, biathlon, bobsledding, mountain biking, and polo. He hasn't gotten to fulfill his dream of being a Formula One race car driver, but to date he has taken nine high-speed driving courses.

Stacie Blair

Founder and CEO of the Pacific Firm, Stacie started her career in executive placement with the prestigious Heidrick & Struggles, but, as she says, "things really fell apart when I rode my motorcycle to the office." This rock climber who likes to go where others have not in both business and sport launched her own placement firm with unique client-centered policies and quickly drove it into the top five in the San Francisco Bay area. She once did an Eco-Challenge race after the fact in Borneo with a few friends just to prove they could do it. Stacie's first career was in military intelligence working for the National Security Agency.

Preston B. Cline

Preston, associate director of the Wharton Leadership Ventures program, is one of the leading experts on risk management in the outdoor field. He began his formal career in the late 1980s, leading 60-day remote wilderness trips with at-risk youth out of New Jersey. Trained as a wilderness emergency medical technician, an NAUI rescue diver, and an ocean lifeguard trainer, Preston has led both terrestrial and marine search and rescue teams. Prior to coming to the Wharton School of the University of Pennsylvania, Preston ran Adventure Management, an operational risk management consulting firm that worked with governments and universities around the world on issues related to teaching and working in remote environments. Preston holds a master's of education degree from the Harvard University Graduate School of Education, Risk and Prevention Program, where he completed formal research in the etymology and epistemology of risk.

Guy Downing

In pursuit of the seven summits, the highest mountains on the seven continents, Guy has in just six years of mountaineering summited Aconcagua in Argentina (22,840

feet), Kilimanjaro in Tanzania (19,339 feet), Mount Elbrus in Russia (18,841 feet), and Vinson Massif in Antarctica (16,067 feet). A veteran of Wall Street investment banking and an alumnus of Stanford Graduate School of Business, he is founder and managing principal, Columbia West Capital. He has executed more than 60 transactions representing a total value topping $25 billion.

Guy Downing, founder and managing principal of Columbia West Capital, in minus 100°F windchill on the 16,067-foot summit of Mt. Vinson, the highest point in Antarctica

Camille Duvall-Hero

A five-time world professional slalom champion water-skier, Camille is managing director at Warburg Realty Partnership in New York and was awarded the Real Estate Board of New York's "Deal of the Year" award in 2002. *Sports Illustrated* named her one of the "100 Greatest Female Athletes of the Century," and she was inducted into the Water Ski Hall of Fame in 2003. Camille has won

15 U.S. waterskiing national titles in her career, reigning as both the world professional slalom champion and U.S. overall champion five times simultaneously. She founded the Professional Association of Water Skiers and was its first president.

Paul Geller

As a litigator and founding partner of a successful Boca Raton law firm, Paul may have been accused of being a pit bull on many occasions, but in reality his expertise in jujitsu has subdued these dogs. In 2008, using the martial arts skills he has honed since boyhood, he thwarted an attack by two pit bulls that put a woman's life at risk—while his proud eight-year-old son watched and called 911 from the car. Paul earned his Juris Doctor degree with highest honors from Emory University School of Law and, after spending several years representing blue chip companies in class action lawsuits at one of the largest corporate defense firms in the world, he became an entrepreneur. He currently heads Coughlin Stoia. He is rated AV by Martindale-Hubbell (the highest rating available) and has served as lead or co–lead counsel in a majority of the securities class actions that have been filed in the southeastern United States in the past several years. Paul is also heavily involved in corporate governance litigation and has successfully represented consumers in class action litigation.

Bob Gordon

As president of Outward Bound Professional, Bob has led the way in delivering experiential programs to corporate and university clients. The company's programs in the areas of team building, leadership development, cultural change, communications, and trust building give Bob a way to share sports that he loves. An avid sailor and mountaineer, he was a member of the 1991 American Karakorum Expedition to Gasherbrum II, also known as K4, and the 13th-highest peak on earth.

Carey Hart

A superstar of freestyle motocross, Carey got hooked at a young age. In 1998 he led the way in making freestyle motocross a sport worth watching and worth money to the people who participated and the companies that sponsored it. He has invented the most extraordinary moves the sport has ever seen, even becoming a featured part of "Ripley's Believe It or Not!" In 2004, Carey's passion for tattoos turned into a business venture that opened in the prestigious Palms Casino in Las Vegas. This move led to another of many TV opportunities for Carey when the A&E network followed the workings of the shop in the reality show "Inked." Carey also opened a club called Wasted Space in June 2008 inside the Hard Rock Casino in Las Vegas.

Gavin Harvey

Gavin, who travels with confidence on his bicycle and motorcycle, but is still working through issues with his fly-fishing, is president and CEO of Versus TV (formerly Outdoor Life Network). He joined Versus from E! Networks, where his leadership in brand development and positioning helped effect the success of E! Entertainment Television, the Style Network, E! International, and E! Online. He holds an M.B.A. from the UCLA Graduate School of Management and an M.A. in international relations from the University of Chicago.

Sharon Kovar

A world-class ultrarunner, Sharon worked in retail for 15 years in every position from entry level to buyer to senior district manager to director of training at the Gap, a position that served as a stepping-stone to her work at Chevron. She created the training network at the Gap for product and sales, starting out as one person with a staff of three and leaving with a staff of 30 in three years. She worked with Ken Blanchard to customize his situational leadership model to the Gap and retrained everyone from executives to store managers on the resulting principles—a unique program for the retailer during a period of transition in which brand consolidation was a dominant concern. Chevron then recruited her to build network and structure around its training organization, especially in its overseas operations. Sometimes this even involved driver's education in countries like Nigeria, Venezuela, and Kazakhstan. She then went to work directly for the chairman of the board, helping him identify leadership competencies of executives to aid in his decisions about moving people to the top tier of Chevron management. She soon became manager of succession planning and development, a position that put her in the middle of all of the senior executives at this $225-plus billion company.

Sophia Le

Sophia is marketing communications manager for Kovarus, a privately held technology consulting firm, and is steadily building her arsenal of skateboarding tricks to help change the perception that her sport is mostly a guy thing.

Diane Leopold

A devotee of "adventure recreation," such as summiting Mt. Kilimanjaro, skiing advanced slopes, and skydiving, Diane has risen at Dominion Resources in a way that reflects her commitment to face challenges methodically. She currently serves as senior vice president of business development and generation construction for this $16 billion power company. She holds a bachelor's degree in electrical and mechanical engineering, a master's in electrical engineering, and an M.B.A. but notes that she did it in spite of the fact that she is bad at math.

Ty Murray

President of Professional Bull Riders, Ty is "King of the Cowboys." He is to rodeo what Wayne Gretzky is to hockey or Michael Jordan is to basketball. In a fifth-grade essay about what he wanted to do when he grew up, he wrote: "I want to beat Larry Mahan's record," referring to the six All-Around World Championships of the rodeo legend who was his hero. After a serious of injuries that delayed his dream by three years, he realized it on December 13, 1998, when he earned a record-breaking seventh All-Around World Championship title. Launched in 1992, the athlete-owned PBR has more than six hundred members in the United States and abroad, and its events broadcast on NBC, Versus TV, and Telemundo currently attract more than six hundred million viewers worldwide.

Deidre Paknad

Deidre is an uphill cyclist with an appetite for the tough ride. As president and CEO of PSS Systems, she drives the solution vision for the leading provider of legal holds and retention management solutions. In 1994 she founded the Compliance Governance and Oversight Council (CGOC), a professional community on retention and preservation, to assemble an ecosystem of domain experts to inform the company's product and market strategies. When she served as CEO of CoVia Technologies, Deidre and the company were inducted into the Smithsonian Institution for Innovation two years in a row.

Julie Pearl

A former competitive skier, as well as a martial arts aficionado during her days at Stanford, Julie founded Pearl Law Group with Alan Nelson, former commissioner of the U.S. Immigration and Naturalization Service, in 1995. Within three years she had developed ImmigrationTracker™, the immigration management system now used by more than 75 percent of top-ranked law firms and many Fortune 1000 companies, hospitals, and universities. Pioneering fresh approaches to customer care—one of which is her policy of fee-based billing rather than the standard per-hour approach in the legal profession—her firm has made "Fastest Growing" lists and was named the number-one woman-owned law firm in the San Francisco Bay area. Julie is a former deputy attorney general in California.

Quang X. Pham

Lathian Health founder and marathoner Quang X. Pham had no CEO experience, no Wall Street experience, no financing experience, and only five years of working in the private sector after he left the United States Marine Corps, and within 14 months of incorporation he had raised $14 million. Naysayers told him not to buck conventional wisdom by spending his valuable time while at the Merage School of Business at University of California, Irvine, writing a "stupid business plan" and entering it in a "dumb contest." That contest was Hummer Winblad Venture Partners' February Madness, from which Quang won $5 million in venture capital with his plan for the world's first virtual drug representative portal. A year later he raised another $9 million. Quang is the author of *A Sense of Duty: My Father, My American Journey.* He flew medivac helicopters for the Marines during Operation Desert Shield.

Mark Richey

Mark is an Alpine-style climber who has done first ascents as well as climbed famous and well-established routes on mountains like Everest. After starting his career making fine musical instruments, he founded and leads Mark Richey Woodworking, a $20 million, Massachusetts-based architectural woodworking firm that employs a hundred people and has won multiple awards related to architectural excellence.

Jeff Roberts

This is a man who loves the fact that flying takes him into surprising environments, requiring him to use skill sets he wouldn't have applications for elsewhere. Jeff was appointed group president, innovation and civil training & services at CAE, in May 2006. While leading CAE's global training organization, with a particular focus on increasing CAE's presence in emerging markets such as India and China, he is also responsible for establishing a company-wide group devoted to innovation. This initiative is intended to identify opportunities for CAE to leverage its expertise and leading-edge technologies in adjacent markets. Previously Jeff had served as group president of CAE's civil business unit. An experienced pilot and training officer, Jeff brings a broad and deep understanding of the aviation training business to his daily work.

Jason Schoonover

Jason is a fellow of the Explorers Club and leader of expedition canoe trips around the world. At a young age he became determined to rise above his economic circumstances and build a life of financial independence so he could spend time canoeing, which he fell in love with at age 10. He carried out his plan by saving his money and investing in real estate; the holdings now make up Schoonover Properties in Canada. As an ethnological field collector, he has contributed pieces to museums around the world as well as to private collections.

Kevin Sheridan

Kevin has an insatiable hunger for travel—he's been to 65 countries—that has included putting one foot in front of the other to reach the summits of the world's highest mountains. He has been known to play guitar and sing at elevations as high as 18,000 feet. As chief executive officer and chief consultant of HR Solutions, Inc., he directs all survey work conducted by the firm. He has extensive experience in the field, having cofounded three successful survey-related organizations. Prior to earning his M.B.A. from Harvard, Kevin spent four years with the Chase Manhattan Bank, N.A., in New York City, London, and Japan. After Harvard, Kevin founded Collegiate Research Services, Inc. (CRS). CRS was established for the sole purpose of introducing the American Career and College Entry Service (ACCES), a unique and cost-free service for high school students in America. Featured in numerous publications including *BusinessWeek* and *USA Today,* ACCES used a survey to create the first electronic link between students and organizations that provide opportunities for further education and training (i.e., post-secondary schools and employers). More than half of all high schools in the country (comprising seven million students) agreed to participate in the service. Kevin grew up on a Native American reservation in northern Wisconsin.

Dennis Sponer

The founder, president, and CEO of ScripNet is a devoted runner and mountain climber who has been named one of Las Vegas's "Top 40 under 40." A lawyer by education, he teamed up with his wife, Jennifer, an M.B.A., to form ScripNet in 1997. The pharmacy benefit manager provides pharmacy management services to worker's compensation companies. ScripNet was named to the Inc. 500 three years in a row, the *Inc.* magazine ranking based on percentage growth in company net sales over a five-year period.

Bob Stangarone

An aerobatics instructor and commercial jet pilot with instrument and multiengine ratings, Bob describes his role as VP corporation communications for Cessna Aircraft Company as "the job I've been looking for all my life." As the lead communications person for the leading manufacturer of general aviation aircraft, he has been responsible for telling the public about some of the most interesting developments and challenges in recent aviation history. Prior to joining Cessna, Bob held the same position with Rolls-Royce North America and Fairchild Dornier and other senior communications positions with Litton and United Technologies' Sikorsky Aircraft and Pratt & Whitney units.

Parks Strobridge

An Ironman triathlete, Parks believes that his sport requires such discipline that the good habits shape his career managing an equity trading desk for Credit Suisse. In short, triathlon is not just a hobby or sport; it's a lifestyle. Parks, who has been with Credit Suisse since 1995, rose through the ranks to run the private bank's equity trading desk.

Kirill Tatarinov

An avid skier drawn to the giant slalom, Kirill, who grew up in Moscow, is the corporate vice president of Microsoft Business Solutions at Microsoft Corp. and oversees the MBS business, with responsibility for sales and marketing, R&D, and operations. MBS develops and markets the line of Microsoft Dynamics products that manage financial, customer relationship, and supply chain management functions for organizations of all sizes. In January 2002, *Computerworld* named Kirill one of the business world's 2002 premier 100 IT leaders. This award honors individuals who have had a positive impact on their organizations through the use of technology. Kirill is a Level-1 ski instructor, certified by the Professional Ski Instructors of America, and teaches skiing through Outdoors for All, programs for people with learning disabilities.

Isabel (Izzy) and Caroline (Coco) Tihanyi

The twin-sister founders of Surf Diva took a passion from their youth and turned it into a surf school and fashion business. Izzy's background as a competitive surfer and surf instructor and Coco's talents in marketing and design converged when they decided to build a business that would support their mutual values and lifestyle. The company now conducts classes in both the United States and Costa Rica.

Bob Travers

Bob's eclectic accomplishments as an athlete/adventurer—from summiting Aconcagua to bicycling around the world to living with goatherds in Kyrgyzstan for three weeks— reflect a sense of exploration that seems out of sync with his role as vice president of wealth management for Citibank. While tackling some of the seven summits, heli- skiing in South America, and earning a ranking of four in his age group in squash doubles, he also managed to build his book of business to the $100 million mark, and it continues to grow. Bob was a pioneer in charging fixed fees based on the amount of assets under management rather than charging clients on a transaction-by-transaction basis.

Cheryl Traverse

The president/CEO of Xceedium is an expedition sailor and scuba diver and now head- ing up her sixth successful start-up. The start-up mentality took hold at the age of 12, when she borrowed some scuba gear to find out what the bottom of a lake looked like. It flourished as she navigated oceans around the world, often in daunting conditions because storms just seem to know where she is sailing. Cheryl pioneered the devel- opment of Xceedium's market position, product portfolio, sales traction, and overall organizational performance. She joined the company from Immunix, where she served as president, CEO, and chairman. Before that she headed Covigo, a mobile middle- ware provider that was purchased by Symbol, and president/CEO of Taviz Technol- ogy, brightinfo.com, which was sold to Annuncio/Peoplesoft. She was EVP with iBand, which Macromedia bought. Cheryl was honored with the TrailBlazer Award in 2002 and the LodeStar Award in 2003 from the Forum for Women Entrepreneurs.

Kristen Ulmer

A former member of the U.S. mogul ski team, Kristen's great love in the sport was the adventure side of it. By the age of 23 she had earned the unofficial title of "best extreme skier in the world" and later accomplished the first female descent of Grand Teton. Kristen currently does executive coaching and conducts clinics for sports and business professionals through her company, Ski to Live. In her work, Kristen captures the inter- section of sports, adventure, and Zen wisdom.

Chris Warner

Chris has summited about 150 times on peaks above 19,000 feet and is one of the most recognized names in mountaineering. He is founder of Earth Treks, Inc., which oper- ates climbing centers, leads expeditions to the world's highest peaks, and partners with the Wharton Leadership Ventures program to take M.B.A. students to peaks in Africa and South America. An American Mountain Guides Association certified alpine guide, Chris has been teaching climbing since 1983. He is the author of *High Altitude Leadership*.

Per Welinder

An internationally acclaimed pioneer in skateboarding, Per took freestyle skateboarding to new heights with his technical prowess before founding Blitz Distribution in 1992. He serves as president of the Huntington Beach, California, company, which handles many of the eight brands he has launched. One of the first was Birdhouse Skateboards, cofounded with Tony Hawk, who purchased 100 percent interest in the company in 2008. Per earned an M.B.A. from UCLA. His current focus is casual apparel for the young male market.

Troy Widgery

Troy is a skydiver, BASE (building, antenna, span, earth) jumper, and founder and president of Go Fast Sports and Beverage Company. A former member of the world-class competitive skydiving team Airmoves, he was among the few survivors of one of the worst plane crashes in skydiving history; after that he founded the company whose first product was a helmet to make skydiving safer. His most recent projects are an energy gum and jet packs that run on relatively affordable fuel and have the potential of becoming a consumer vehicle. Troy's first jet pack made its debut in the summer of 2008 with 33 seconds of continuous flight, and his forthcoming high-end model will provide nine minutes of continuous flight.

John Wilson

John runs the gamut in outdoor adventure, from climbing the world's highest mountains to motorcycling through 26 countries—a 25,000-mile trip—to fly-fishing. He is founder, president, and CEO of J.C. Wilson Associates, a San Francisco–based executive search firm specializing in searches for the financial services, advanced technology, and biotech industries. His early career, when the mountaineering urge grabbed him, involved making significant loan recommendations for Citibank in Hong Kong, Malaysia, and Singapore.

Gord Woolley

Gord is founder and president of Jessam Communications, a graphic arts and design company, and a former member of the Canadian Olympic bobsled team. He became the brakeman by default when his teammate, Kirby Best (see earlier entry), told him how to handle his job: "When I scream 'brakes,' put the damn things on." Named to the Olympic team, he had a horrific accident in sled number 13, 13th position, 13th turn. It prevented him from competing in the Sarajevo games, but it did not make him superstitious.

Operational Concepts

Actual Risk: The true level of risk with risk mitigation and success enhancement measures taken into account. The same risk without proposed risk mitigation and success enhancement actions taken into account is the *perceived risk*.

Areas for Improvement: One of three categories into which a person's capabilities are sorted in determining his or her *natural skill set*. Areas for improvement are the tasks and skills for which ability is low. The other two categories are *strengths* and *serviceable skills*. (Also see *weaknesses*.)

Avoided Risk: A risk a person has determined to be unnecessary or undesirable for his or her normal functioning. Avoided risks are not fixed and vary with time.

Best-Case Outcome: The most desirable outcome that can result from a course of action.

Calling: The role to which a person's *natural skill set*, *passions*, and *purpose* make him or her ideally suited.

Career Risks: Risks such as pursuing job changes, taking on new responsibilities, and seeking promotions.

Chosen Risk: A risk a person has determined is required for him or her to function. Such determination is not necessarily a result of conscious assessment.

Comfort Threshold: The limit of a person's *comfort zone*. Moving beyond the comfort threshold will take a person out of his or her *comfort zone*. On the *spectrum of all risks*, the comfort threshold is the point between *optional risks* and *avoided risks*.

Comfort Zone: The realm within which a person feels comfortable functioning.

Compound Rewards: The rewards that cannot be identified when a risk is being considered. As a result, they are the unanticipated rewards.

Creative Risks: Risks such as painting, drawing, taking on a writing challenge, and pursuing an unconventional design.

Direct Rewards: The rewards that can be identified when a risk is being considered and as a result will strongly influence the decision as to whether to take the risk.

Disaster Check: One of the finals steps in the risk assessment and success enhancement process. The disaster check involves evaluating the acceptability of any undesirable outcomes. A wholly unacceptable outcome dictates a decision not to proceed and hence avoid a "disaster."

Dream Job: A job that fully engages a person's *natural skill set* and *passions*.

Emotional Fear: A fear that is gut driven and instinctive but not necessarily based on fact. The alternative is a *mental fear* that is mind driven, rational, and based on fact.

Emotional Risks: Risks that require a person to be emotionally vulnerable.

Financial Risks: A person's risk tolerance in activities such as investing, borrowing, and lending money.

Gift of Mortality: A person's awareness and resulting actions based on the knowledge that his or her life is of finite duration.

Intellectual Risks: Risks such as a person's willingness to study a difficult topic, pursue information that challenges his or her convictions, or read an intellectually challenging book.

Intermediate Outcome: A possible outcome from a risk that falls between the *best-case* and the *worst-case outcome*.

Invalid Fear: A fear that is not supported by facts or circumstances and is as a result invalid.

Mental Fear: A fear that is mind driven, rational, and based on fact. The alternative is an *emotional fear*, which is gut driven and instinctive but not necessarily based on fact.

Natural Skill Set: An assessment of a person's innate abilities as they are sorted into three categories based on ability and level of fulfillment. The three categories are *strengths, serviceable skills,* and *areas for improvement* or *weaknesses*.

Opportunity Territory: The area beyond a person's *comfort zone* in which he or she will find opportunities not yet taken. On the *spectrum of all risks*, the opportunity territory is the area to the right of the line between *optional risks* and *avoided risks*.

Optional Risk: A risk a person has decided to take even though it is not required for him or her to function.

Passion: A person's deeply held desires, concerns, and beliefs.

Passion/Life Nexus: The extent to which a person has brought his or her passions and life structure into alignment.

Perceived Risk: The perceived level of risk without risk mitigation and success enhancement measures taken into account. The same risk when revised by taking proposed risk mitigation and success enhancement actions into account is the *actual risk*.

Personal Risk Inclination: A person's self-assessed risk inclination ranked on a scale of 1 to 10 with 1 being very risk averse and 10 being very risk inclined.

Physical Risks: Activities that involve some risk of injury such as motorcycle riding, river rafting, rock climbing, or skydiving.

Possible Outcome: An outcome that could result from a certain course of action.

Possible Outcomes Matrix: A matrix that contains all possible outcomes being assessed in order from most to least desirable with the corresponding likelihood of each possible outcome presented as a percentage.

Purpose: A person's perception of his or her reason for being.

Reality Check: Assessing the validity of fears triggered by a possible course of action.

Risk: Any action with an undetermined outcome.

Risk Quotient (RQ): A numerical indication of a person's current risk inclination over a broad range of risk types that is derived from self-assessment. RQs fall between 1 and 10 with 1 being very risk averse and 10 being very risk inclined.

Serviceable Skills: One of three categories into which a person's capabilities are sorted in determining his or her *natural skill set*. Serviceable skills are the tasks and skills for which ability is high but fulfillment is low. The other two categories are *strengths* and *areas for improvement* or *weaknesses*.

Spectrum of All Risks: A graphic representation of the spectrum of all risks a person can contemplate, ranging from the least risky actions on the left to the most risky actions on the right. The risk categories on the spectrum fit into one of three categories: *chosen*, *optional*, and *avoided*.

Strength/Weakness Paradox: The premise that a positive trait, if applied in the extreme, can become negative.

Strengths: One of three categories into which a person's capabilities are sorted in determining a *natural skill set*. Strengths are the tasks and skills for which both ability and fulfillment are high. The other two categories are *serviceable skills* and *areas for improvement* or *weaknesses*.

Turning Points: Significant events that change the direction of a person's life.

Unsupported Fear: A fear that is not supported by facts or circumstances and is as a result unsupportable.

Valid Fear: A fear that is supported by facts or circumstances and is as a result valid.

Weaknesses: One of three categories into which a person's capabilities are sorted in determining his or her *natural skill set*. Weaknesses are the tasks and skills for which ability is low. The other two categories are *strengths* and *serviceable skills*. (Also see *areas for improvement*.)

Worst-Case Outcome: The least desirable outcome that can result from a certain course of action.

Index